CREATING A LIFE OF ABUNDANCE

A Couple's Journey Together in Business, Real Estate and Short-term Rentals

Andrew Hanson, Meghan Douglas Hanson
Steve Duffley, Christine Duffley
Ryan Duffy, Shae Duffy
Dave Menapace and Kim Menapace

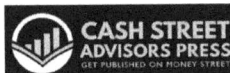

CASH STREET ADVISORS PRESS
GET PUBLISHED ON MONEY STREET

First published in 2023 by Cash Street Advisors Press LLC

ISBN # Paper: 979-8-9887875-0-1
ISBN #EBook: 979-8-9887875-2-5
Library of Congress Control Number: 2023915294
Printed in the United States of America

Editing by James Douglas
Formatting and cover design by Kristina Conatser
www.capturedbykcdesigns.com

Disclaimer:
The information in this book is for educational purposes only. This book is intended to provide reliable and competent information regarding its subject matter, but it is not intended to be a source of financial or legal advice. The Author and publisher are not engaged in providing legal, financial or other professional advisory services. Please note that laws and practices often vary from state to state and from country to country, and any important legal or financial decisions should only be made after consulting a licensed professional. The author and publisher make no guarantees of any financial or legal results that may be obtained by using this book. The author and publisher specifically disclaim responsibility for any losses or liability that may arise from the use or application of this book's contents.

DEDICATION

To all the couples who dare to dream together, who navigate both love's tender embrace and the tumultuous world of entrepreneurship hand in hand. This book is dedicated to you—the visionary couples in business together. Your unwavering commitment to each other and your shared vision is an inspiration to us all.

May "Creating a Life of Abundance" serve as a guiding light on your journey, reminding you that love, and partnership are the cornerstones of both a flourishing relationship and a thriving business. Here's to your unbreakable bond and the abundance you create together.

TABLE OF CONTENTS

INTRODUCTION

Welcome to the world of "Creating a Life of Abundance"–a heartfelt journey that beckons you into the lives of four incredible couples, each with a unique story to tell, including the visionary authors themselves, Andrew and Meghan Hanson. Here, the pages are not just paper and ink; they're windows into the human spirit's boundless capacity for growth, connection, and dreams fulfilled. This isn't your typical self-help book, nor is it a collection of success stories meant to intimidate. No, this is a gathering of stories that hum with the energy of relatability, vulnerability, and authenticity.

As you read about Andrew and Meghan's own trials, triumphs, and the love that holds them steady, you'll realize that the pursuit of abundance isn't an abstract concept–it's a journey that weaves through the messy, beautiful realities of life. But this book isn't just about the Hanson's. It's a celebration of people who refused to settle for mediocrity and chose, instead, to sculpt lives that resonate with purpose.

You'll meet Dave and Kim, the youngest couple, who embark on a journey of both parenthood and entrepreneurship. With their hands full balancing a growing family and a budding business, they discover the extraordinary strength that comes from supporting one another's dreams.

Ryan and Shae's bond has been tested by the trials of life, yet their relationship has emerged unbreakable. Their story is one of perseverance, proving that true love can weather any storm and grow stronger through every challenge.

Steve and Christine, the embodiment of dedication, infuse their business with humanity. Their unwavering commitment to their craft and their genuine care for the people around them illuminate the path to success paved with authenticity and empathy.

As you turn these pages, you'll walk alongside these couples–their laughter, their tears, and their unyielding spirit to become your companions. They remind us that abundance isn't just about material wealth; it's about embracing every facet of life–the highs and lows, the love and loss–and weaving them into a tapestry that's uniquely ours.

So, let this book be more than words on paper. Let it be an invitation to explore your own dreams, to face your challenges head-on, and to find abundance in the most unexpected corners of your life.

With open hearts, Andrew and Meghan Hanson, along with our fellow storytellers, offer you a glimpse into lives that have been touched by the extraordinary. And as you journey with us, may you discover the extraordinary within yourself.

CREATING AN ABUNDANT LIFESTYLE TOGETHER

BY ANDREW AND MEGHAN HANSON

"Partnership is not a legal contract between two equal individuals. It's an emotional alliance between two people who are committed to each other's success."
– Warren Buffet, businessman, investor, and philanthropist

As the title of the book suggests, creating an abundance lifestyle together with your spouse is extremely important in business and all other endeavors in life and family. My name is Andrew Hanson, my wife's name is Meghan and we are both entrepreneurial and extremely passionate about all things real estate, investing, banking, hospitality, small business and, most recently, our newfound passion for writing and teaching others about financial freedom and investing in real estate. We live in a small rural town in the beautiful Lake Sunapee Region of New Hampshire, USA. If you're not familiar with New Hampshire, it's a vacationer's paradise, with all four seasons packed full of recreation activity and an abundance of outdoor space, wildlife and state parks to enjoy. But we did not always live in New Hampshire. Meghan and I have been extremely private with our journey, personal lives, and struggles. We have built our lives together, slowly working our way up to be top real estate investors, local small business owners, and community non-profit leaders.

"The Master Mind principle: Two or more people actively engaged in the pursuit of a definite purpose with a positive mental attitude, constitute an unbeatable force."
– Napoleon Hill

We currently own and operate several successful companies in the great state of New Hampshire. But our journey hasn't been easy, and we've had our share of heartache. For the first time, Meghan and I will talk about some of our most vulnerable moments and some of our wins. We have discovered during our twenty-three years of life together that breaking down barriers, working hard, holding faith in each other, and never giving up are essential in business and in life. We hope by sharing our story we can inspire other couples to rise together, no matter their backgrounds, to the top. If you dream big, and work hard together, you can achieve a life of abundance! We hope you, the reader, will benefit from reading our story.

"To me, a spouse should be a life partner AND a business partner. Just like any good partner, her strengths must make up for my weaknesses and vice versa."
– Robert Kiyosaki, entrepreneur, and author

HERE'S A LITTLE BIT ABOUT OUR STORY
STARTING OUT TOGETHER

Meghan and I grew up on the South Shore of Massachusetts, although we did not live in the same town. We met through mutual friends at the time. I was sixteen years old and Meghan was fifteen. This was back in the days when your friend handed you a picture of someone that they knew was available to hook up. When I was handed the picture of Meghan, I saw a beautiful, young girl that totally captured my eyes and my heart and I was tremendously excited to meet her. A few weeks later, we met at a party in Brockton, Massachusetts at my friend's apartment. There were so many people at the party, I lost track of Meghan. A fight broke out, and I threw some punches to defend myself. It was a chaotic scene and I remember seeing Meghan crying. She was afraid. So, I went over and comforted her. I asked if she wanted to come over the next day and watch the Patriots game. She agreed!

After getting to know each other, we truly became best friends. We did everything together. Slowly, we started ditching our friends, working towards our dreams, and looking for our opportunity to make our own path out in the world together. Meghan and I both come from humble family backgrounds. Meghan grew up in a low-income family with her mom making only ten thousand dollars a year. My parents were lower middle-class, blue-collar workers. We both had parents that got divorced when we were younger, which was something that helped us understand each other a bit more. We love our parents very much, and they have taught us tremendous skills, but they were more living life by a survival mindset rather than an abundance mindset when we were growing up. But they sure did teach us how to be survivors.

We spent a lot of time at my mom's house hanging out after work and on the weekends. I was living there in the basement and Meghan and I would spend time there. We both worked hard. I would work from 5:00 am to about 7:00 pm or later as I was a laborer for a local fence company. Meghan and I would spend the weekends together searching for land lots in New Hampshire. On top of that we were always hanging out with Meghan's nephew Jimmy.

Jimmy was born when Meghan was nine years old. Meghan's oldest sister was sixteen when she got pregnant. So, they have a unique bond where they are aunt and nephew, sister and brother, mother and son. Jimmy was six years old the first time I met him as he was living under Meghan's mom's care at their home. He and Meghan were very close and because of that connection the three of us spent a lot of time together. Plus, Jimmy and I were only ten years apart, making me one very cool uncle to be around! In fact, the three of us still get together to this day and the connection is stronger than ever. I truly enjoyed my time with these two. They were the dose of life I needed. They gave me faith, unconditional love, and a reason to keep pushing forward. We would also hang out as much as possible with our niece and other nephews and enjoy each other's company. We dreamed big together, thinking of all the amazing possibilities life had to offer us.

Tragically, when Meghan was seventeen, she lost her dad to suicide. Although Meghan and I had met only a year prior and had been enjoying each other's company, I'm not sure anything could have prepared us for this life-changing event. Meghan was over at my house when the phone call came through. It was her mom, you could tell it was urgent from the tone of her voice, but it was also vague. "You need to come home right now", her mother insisted.

Meghan could feel the anxiety building and we could both tell something was wrong. I told her that things would be ok and we got in the car and headed to her mother's house We talked throughout what seemed like a never-ending drive, although her house was only thirty-minutes away. We speculated maybe something happened to her grandfather or maybe her nephew Jimmy got injured, both of whom she was extremely close to. We weren't prepared for the reality. It didn't look good when we arrived at the house. Her mother was waiting for us inside, her face grim. Meghan was told that her dad had attempted suicide and was currently in a New Hampshire Hospital on critical life support. It was a devastating and tragic event. The toughest part of that day was having to go home and leave Meghan behind to grieve and process all that was happening by herself. When we heard we were able to visit her dad in the hospital, we immediately drove to New Hampshire. Meghan was able to see him, one last time, but with tubes and wires everywhere trying to keep him alive. Tragically, Meghan's dad "Skip" passed away a few days later. Meghan suffered a tremendous loss, and I never got the chance to meet her dad, which was unfortunate and something that will always bother me. I wanted to gain his trust and approval as I truly love his daughter and love her more each day. It was such a traumatic time in Meghan's life. Meghan struggled to focus in school and as a result was tutored out of school her senior year in high school. With her extreme strength, she persevered and was able to graduate with her class.

As for me, I was already out in the workforce as a laborer working in construction. Luckily, because I had worked various construction jobs with my dad throughout the years, that was what I knew best. I was a hands-on worker, working my ass off about ten to twelve hours a day. It was hard work, but laborer was pretty much what I qualified for as a 16-year-old high school dropout and didn't come from a connected family. There's not enough room in this chapter to dive into my high school years and parents' divorce, I couldn't hang on my last year in high school. I just couldn't take it anymore. I had already been a runaway kid twice during my high school years, had big gaps in my education, had the state involved in my life, and I was being bottled up eight hours a day in the ALP. They called it the 'Alternative Learning Program' and it was very tough for me. It was a rough classroom environment, full of the school's problem students. Honestly, it was so disruptive that it did more harm than good. I couldn't get out soon enough.

After Meghan graduated high school, she wanted to get right out on her own and out of her home environment. We decided to move in with my dad, who owned a two-family apartment building. All three of us lived in the main house while he continued to rent out the other half to long term tenants. Before my parents got divorced and lost everything, my mom and dad owned a multi-family so I was used to the landlord environment when I was very young. My dad split the rent and all the bills in thirds, it worked out perfectly. I was employed at Creative Playthings as lead foreman in their construction landscape division. I was in charge of the employees, estimating, and heavy equipment. Our job was to build and install play pits and safe play areas for playgrounds. After a few years, I became a sub-contractor for the company. And that's when my first company was born! I was responsible for hiring my own employees, purchasing vehicles and equipment, completing the jobs, obtaining customer satisfaction, invoicing, and bookkeeping.

At this time Meghan was attending a community college part-time, taking courses in accounting and business. She was working as much as she could part-time at a healthcare clinic while being my bookkeeper on the side. We kept our money separate, had our own checking accounts, worked and saved money. We were learning valuable skills working together and managing the landscape company I had created. I always had so much support from Meghan and she believed in my big dreams.

Under the age of twenty, we already had a dump truck, heavy equipment, and a 12'x12' shed full of tools. I was still operating out of my dad's house, plus we were helping him maintain the apartment building, and completing several projects together.

I had friends, family, and many people working for me at that time in our lives. But we were faced with so much criticism about our dreams, the business I was creating, wanting to purchase land up north, and our relationship. I think part of the reason we were searching in New Hampshire for land was a way for Meghan to reconnect with her dad, as he loved fishing and living on a tiny pond in New Hampshire.

THE MOMENT WHEN YOUR REALITY AND WHY GET STRONGER

As we look back writing this chapter, we both realize this was a turning point in our lives. Our reality was changing and our lives had a different trajectory than those around us. While our friends were getting bogged down with kids, drinking, or even drugs, we were focusing on the business and saving money to move up north. I was landing and completing five-to-ten-thousand-dollar jobs, and Meghan was helping me keep the books. We had many critics and skeptics in our lives, doubting our dreams and testing our resolve. We ignored them, choosing instead to look towards a brighter future and believe in our big dreams. Our path took us away from the *I can't* and the *that's not possible* and led us to accomplish our goals.

After many weekend trips to New Hampshire searching for land, we came across a 10-acre land lot. Late one winter afternoon, we drove to the property, parked on the side of the road, jumped over the tall snowbank and started walking up the long steep driveway in waist high snow. When we reached the peak and looked around, we knew this was the one. It was a large corner lot with over 1,000 feet of road frontage, 600 feet from a lake boat launch, and it had power going to a little cabin on top of the hill. *What more could we ask for?*

We immediately drove to the real estate agent's office and submitted an offer. It was an exciting and scary experience for us. We negotiated the purchase of the land in another state, without our parents or a buyer's agent (what is that?). We had no clue! A deposit was put down and we excitedly drove the two and a half hours back to Massachusetts! Our next mission was obtaining financing. *Where do we start? Would someone believe in us?*

Meghan was eighteen and I was nineteen years old. I owned a construction and landscape company that was doing well, but I was still very young, self-employed, just started the business, and as a result we were thrown into a high-risk category by the banks. Meghan was still attending a community college, while working at a healthcare clinic part-time, and we were living at my dad's. Grabbing the phone book, we started searching for banks to apply at.

After calling what seemed to be every bank in New Hampshire, we finally found a local bank willing to work with us. We received approval, but there were certain conditions that needed to be met. One was finding a co-signer for the loan as we did not have enough credit history. Although we were young, we knew how important credit was through the equipment loans. We did not give it much thought when we took the leap of faith on this land purchase. This was a great lesson on how important having and building credit when you are younger is.

While we were met with temporary defeat, we put our heads together and approached the one person we knew would believe in our mission and in our characters: my dad. He agreed to be our co-signer as we had never missed a rent payment with him. This was such an exciting time for me and Meghan. Our very first loan was for land in New Hampshire, two and a half hours away from our house. We put 30% down and financed 70%. It was truly a huge opportunity and learning experience for us.

On top of our first real estate purchase together, the results of our hard work led to us dreaming of our future in New Hampshire.

We would head up to New Hampshire every weekend, either by ourselves or with family, and work on the land. We cleared trees, put in a driveway, a huge fire pit, and a culvert. It was a great place to camp out and experience New Hampshire. We weren't ready to move yet, but were chomping at the bit to start our life there.

Camp Unity

ENVISIONING OUR FAMILY'S FUTURE DREAMS

While we were still living at my dad's house, he allowed us to purchase our first dog, Joscelyn, an English bulldog. We were so excited to start our family! Although it doesn't seem like a big deal for a couple to own a dog, it was a huge responsibility. We had just gotten in a routine with ourselves being in a relationship, living together full time, purchasing land, signing a loan together and now we had to get in a routine with the dog. She was our baby. That same year, when Meghan was twenty-one years old and I was twenty-two, with our family started, we decided we were ready to move out of my dad's and find a house. We were young and ready for a new start together. We searched the South Shore of Massachusetts, but with its expensive cost of living and high-priced homes, we soon looked elsewhere. We looked towards New Hampshire with its tremendous wildlife, year-round outdoor recreation activities, and large lake regions. The free-spirited lifestyle of the New Hampshire citizens intrigued us. However, we had a decision to make. *Do we build on our land lot or do we buy a house? What about the business?*

After outlining the pros and cons of each option, we decided to purchase a house. We loaded up the car with our dog and headed back up to New Hampshire. It only took us three properties to walk through before we found our home. Our excitement shined as brightly as the sunshine pouring into the kitchen of the new house. Yet again, we followed the realtor to her office and put in an offer. No calling our parents for advice. No sleeping on it. We were ready to make this house our home. Our offer was accepted, which included the seller contributing three percent towards our closing costs. We were so excited to be purchasing our first house together!

Next came pulling out the phone book and calling banks to qualify us for this home loan. It seemed as though everyone was against us. Nothing was working out, people around us started spreading seeds of doubt. Although we already had a loan and didn't miss a payment, we still didn't have enough credit history to obtain an approval. It was so frustrating. We were so close to having our own home, but our lack of credit history was slowing us down. Meghan was finally able to speak with someone at a local mortgage company who was willing to offer us an 80/20 loan. Basically 100% financing, split into two loans. One loan would be for eighty percent of the purchase price and at a lower interest rate, the other loan would be for twenty percent of the purchase price at a higher interest rate. The mortgage company assured us no bank would even consider us due to our lack of credit history. With my self-employment and Meghan's part-time job, they said they were our only option. Feeling defeated and ready to sign on the dotted line with the mortgage company, Meghan called one more bank. A local bank was offering a first-time home buyers' program, where we would only need to put three percent of the purchase price down and the bank would finance the rest. This was the break we needed. We quickly completed the application and were shortly approved thereafter. One of our strongest assets is our perseverance. This lesson taught us to contact local banks and credit unions, as they'll often be more willing to work with you and listen to your dreams and goals.

We loaded up the dog and a U-Haul and drove to New Hampshire, where our new life together as a family began. We had no family in the area, only one local friend, we had no jobs, and only $3,000 in our savings account left after the down payment on our first house. We had plenty of construction equipment. My hard work had paid off in many ways. I had a few jobs on the books and was willing to travel back and forth to Massachusetts to fit in all our clients and to keep us afloat. Looking back, we took a huge risk at a new beginning for our lives in New Hampshire and are very glad that we did.

DIVING DEEPER INTO OUR PERSONAL AND PROFESSIONAL JOURNEY

When we arrived in New Hampshire, I soon found an entry-level job as a maintenance technician. I needed a more solid foundation as I got started in a new state. It was a great steady job with full benefits, plus I could still work construction on the weekends. I was truly fortunate to be working with experienced maintenance technicians overseeing 1,500 to 1,800 rental units. We serviced everything from senior housing, large multi-family complexes, student housing, commercial real estate, industrial spaces, and high-quality vacation homes in the Vermont and New Hampshire mountains.

At that same time Meghan had a similar start to her career, starting out in an entry-level position at a local bank in their file room. Her thirst for knowledge allowed her to quickly progress through the bank in small steps, one year at a time. Each position she held gave her deep insight into the inner workings of the banking industry and real estate, as well as teaching her lessons we would use years down the road.

We were your average nine to five employees, saving for home projects, weekend getaways, and our upcoming dream wedding. We continued to be entrepreneurial and landed small jobs for my construction company and would complete them after hours and on the weekends. During the winter months, I did whatever I could on the side including using my ATV to plow neighbors' driveways and for the elderly at a local mobile home park while Meghan shoveled the walkways. We always worked as a team on all the projects. Because of my skills and knowledge in construction, Meghan and I were able to perform projects around our house, including adding a deck, installing a new roof, adding a patio, installing attic collar ties and an attic stairway, tiling floors, adding fencing, and building our first chicken coop among the countless other light carpentry side projects.

Everything was going great, but we struggled. We had big dreams but also had two mortgages to pay for, our home and the land lot. We had to take full responsibility for ourselves, paying bills, grocery shopping and trying to save money was difficult. Although New Hampshire was only one state away from Massachusetts, we underestimated the environment. We didn't realize we would need snow tires for our vehicles, which was an added expense we weren't planning for. Additional house maintenance, like raking the snow off the house roof after every snowstorm, the amount of oil we needed to get through the long winters, and the countless 'oh no' moments that had drained our savings account rapidly. We learned a lot together and continued to adapt and change to the new environment. During the long New Hampshire winters, we would only fill up the oil tank with funds left over after all our bills were paid. To conserve, we would shut down rooms in the house and keep the heat set at the lowest tolerable temperature. I was lucky to get the heat above 60 degrees. We had extra blankets everywhere and baked in the oven a lot. We were just scraping by.

After settling into our new home, we decided to add a new addition to our family, a Hurricane Katrina rescue dog named Pinto Bean. He was an amazing dog! Not only did he bring joy into our lives, but he also brought joy to everyone he met. Our niece and nephews loved him. We loved to have our niece and nephews come up and visit for weekends or school vacations. We would seek out an adventure or experience with them that would create lasting memories. We would play Mario Kart on the Nintendo 64 and talk about the endless possibilities in life. We mostly tried to teach them love and that anything was possible. That if they worked hard, they could do anything. It was important for us to stay close to them, even though we now lived 150 miles away. We were constantly doing things and having fun with them. As we didn't have children, our niece and nephews got spoiled. Our motto was 'no rules, just right'. But Meghan ensured we did have rules and structure. Even though we were young, we were instilling morals, ethics, and sound values into these children. We thought differently than our peers and we wanted to show the kids another point of view.

EMBRACING OUR VOWS AND FAMILY COMMITMENT AMIDST THE BEAUTY OF HAWAII

In 2007, Meghan and I fully committed to each other and got engaged. As I could not obtain Meghan's dad's permission to marry his daughter, I asked the next best man in her life, her grandfather, Andy. Boy was he a character. He was a Sicilian who told me the first time I met him "Spaghetti or Revenge. You mess with my granddaughter, it's revenge!". He also told me of his extended family that was from the Dorchester, Massachusetts area. Thankfully, I was always on his good side. With his approval and full blessing, we and thirteen family members all boarded a plane and took the eighteen-hour journey to Hawaii where Meghan and I said our vows and got maui'ed! It wasn't until this point in our relationship that we started combining our bank accounts and income together. We had gone seven years before committing even further to our togetherness. I think a part of our hesitation was that we both had come from divorced families. But after seven years we knew we were soulmates, and we were not looking back. This was another major milestone in our lives where we decided to join forces and manage our money together.

Surrounded by family on Ka'anapali Beach, Lahaina Maui

When we got back from Hawaii, it was back to reality for us. Winter didn't wait for us. The oil tank needed a fill, and after a fourteen-day vacation, our employers were eager to have us return. It was back to the maintenance grind for me but looking back, I realize that having many years in this role as a hands-on certified maintenance technician was excellent exposure to the importance of maintaining your assets. Despite everything going on in my personal life, my job taught me the inner workings of maintenance operations, property management in a wide variety of sectors, maintaining and protecting assets, and the relationship between proper facility maintenance, and being successful at owning real estate assets. I also learned one of the biggest lessons of real estate early on; proper people management. I was drained, it was hard work! I was the new guy, so I was on call on holidays and twenty-four hours for emergencies. The calls would come at the worst times, interrupting my home life and preventing me from having weekends or even going to family events. I lost a lot of time with Meghan at home.

Many times, Meghan would ride along and keep me company on the service call. It was a pleasure having her there, in each other's company, even though our time together was interrupted with work. Not only did I get a tremendous amount of insight into the true work it takes to properly maintain real estate assets; Meghan was also gaining that same insight through my career experience.

After many years as a hands-on technician, I worked my way up to becoming a hands-on property manager of a 144-unit condominium complex in my local community. From there, with a support team of employees that trusted my leadership, I soon progressed to a property manager of several complexes throughout the state. In total, I was managing over 350 rental units, a $38 million portfolio in the state of New Hampshire. My reality was expanding faster and faster.

Being exposed to real estate on this level was a major milestone in my life. I was listening to audio books as I managed a staff of 14 and multi-million dollars of real estate. I was exposed to my boss's structure of multiple companies all in different sectors of the industries he was in. He owned a large drilling and blasting construction company, a company that sold products to the drilling and blasting industry, and an equipment corporation selling the heavy equipment and supplies, all while owning and managing a massive two generational real estate portfolio spanning across the entire US.

Having lunches with my boss, I learned his father came from a background similar to mine; his father also did not finish high school. From basic beginnings, his father built the portfolio of real estate and family of companies all off the fruits of labor from his construction company. This exposure to my boss and his mindset led me to develop my own mindset, adopting his methods and learning from his family. Even then, he could see I was on the path to make a brighter future for my family through business and real estate and I am beyond honored to have worked for them. I was truly exposed to the velocity of money.

Meghan was focusing on her career at the bank. She was taking on various roles at the bank, from Loan Servicer to Senior Commercial Lending Assistant. She gained extensive knowledge on business and commercial loan documentation, entity structure, and risk mitigation. While doing all of this, Meghan was also taking courses on various banking topics to further her career and was cross trained in other departments. She was responsible for making sure the due diligence was done on every loan transaction. From appraisals, legal and title work, environmental, financial, preparing loan documentation, and the back-end inputs of loans into the banking system, Meghan saw to it that everything was done.

Her curiosity and her professionalism led to her learning from many senior colleagues and attorneys. These experiences gave her valuable insight into the importance of entity structure, loan structuring for large corporations and real estate investors, and succession plans for multi-million-dollar legacies. In addition to the insight, this information started to expand Meghan's reality.

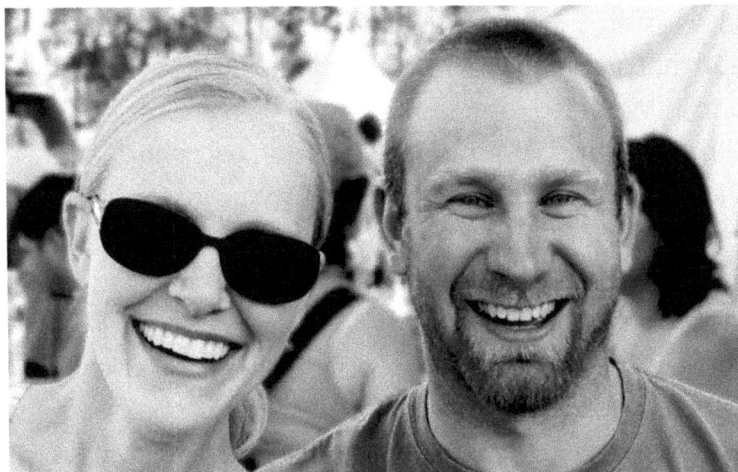

Quechee Vermont Balloon Festival, Photo taken by Tiffany Hall, a great friend

THE ABUNDANCE MINDSET FOR FINANCIAL
AND TIME FREEDOM TOGETHER

While I was still working as a property manager for W-2 income, I had a strong, burning desire to become financially free for my family's future after everything I had been exposed to from my boss. A vendor I was using handed me the book, *Rich Dad Poor Dad* by Robert T Kiyosaki. That book, followed by many others in the *Rich Dad Advisors* series, has helped shape my outlook and allowed me to develop a mindset of abundance as an entrepreneur and small business owner. That desire, combined with my reputation as a successful property manager, community-driven leader, and my deep passion for real estate, led me to form CITYSCAPE LLC in 2011 with that same vendor, Jason.

Jason and I had started the company as an investment company to buy and hold a few assets for cash flow while also doing a few fix and flip transactions each year. It didn't take long before Cityscape was growing fast and, with everything Meghan and I had learned, it became evident that we needed to separate its mission before too long.

As a result, two companies were formed to provide better entity structure: a service company and a real estate holding company. We also started to take on more construction, development and maintenance work, growing the service company's sales. During this time, I was receiving words of caution from family members about my business partner. "Couldn't I do this on my own?" and "You're going to get burnt", the naysayers said.

I was working late hours on my own business and felt exhausted a lot of the time. I left Meghan alone, a lot. I would come home after work, eat supper with Meghan, and then head out to work the *night shift*. The night shift entailed me physically remodeling the fix and flips I had purchased. I also had to catch up with the crews or vendors so they could complete their work during the day or ensure the next phase of the job site was ready when they showed up in the morning. The night shift and weekends were my only chance to work on my own business.

Overcoming the solitude was a large hurdle for Meghan to get over, especially when we did everything together. I had reprogrammed my mindset for the life of abundance while Meghan, although she trusted me with this new venture, was still trying to change her reality to keep up with mine.

While nurturing the growth of my businesses, Meghan and I dedicated ourselves to a shared mission of financial freedom and generational wealth. Drawing from our collective background in real estate, we embarked on this joint endeavor. We created our first LLC and moved our first house into it, renting it out long term while we moved into a four-unit multi-family property my holding company owned. We sacrificed for many years, but we were dedicated to our financial freedom. We moved from investment property to investment property as we searched for our new home. Our friends call us "the masters of delayed gratification", but given our roots it comes naturally to us. Simultaneously, I had the privilege of serving as a director on various nonprofit boards within my community. These roles not only allowed me to give back to the community I cherished but also refined my skills in strategic planning and collaboration with brilliant minds. A pinnacle moment arrived at the age of twenty-eight when I was recognized as the Young Professional of the Year by the Claremont Chamber of Commerce. This experience proved invaluable, as the principles and strategies I employed while serving on these boards seamlessly translated into the realm of my businesses.

On the entrepreneurial front, our progress was gaining momentum, We found ourselves overseeing the maintenance and rehabilitation of an impressive 100-200 foreclosed properties per year across New Hampshire and Vermont. The aftermath of the 2008 financial crisis had resulted in a surge of foreclosures, consequently creating a micro economy within our local communities. Investors, much like ourselves, capitalized on extraordinary real estate opportunities, procuring homes for mere fractions of their market value. During a routine trash out estimate on a two-family that was owned by an out of state asset management company, I was able to purchase the cheapest property in my career! I had submitted a trash out estimate for $2,900.00. Later that day, I received a call from the asset management company asking if I would be willing to purchase the two-family house for the estimated price. I was speechless, but quickly composed myself, it was a no-brainer, and accepted his offer!

While I felt like I was on top of the world, I was hit with a back injury at work. We were working on a new fire alarm system for the entire six building complex I was managing. It was a fairly large capital improvement project costing around $476,000. We subcontracted the majority of the work but me and the maintenance staff were building the fire alarm panel station outside. I was setting 6x6's in concrete Sono Tubes. It happened fast. As soon as I pulled the bag of concrete out of the truck, I felt something in my back. It was a quick sharp pain, I ignored, and continued working the rest of the day. The next day I could barely move. This began a major setback in my life physically. I was in incredible pain. I had injured my thoracic spine. It was hard to do any physical or vigorous work. Then it was countless doctors, physical therapy sessions, MRI's, orthopedic options, and pain management.

During my period of light duty at work, my nature as a hands-on and high-energy individual became quite evident. Adapting to the constraints of light duty proved to be quite challenging for someone like me. The injury I had sustained undoubtedly forced me to decelerate, and for a while, I felt a sense of setback.

Embracing this unexpected downtime, I recognized an opportunity to transition into a more managerial role. My innate thirst for knowledge and constant desire to elevate my career in property management steered me in a fresh direction. As I embarked on this journey of growth, I seized the chance to earn a series of real estate management certificates offered by the prestigious Institute of Real Estate Management. This pursuit underscored my commitment as a lifelong learner, propelling me forward on the path to further professional advancement.

While Meghan and I continued to move from investment property to investment property, in 2013, we had finally found the right place to call home. It was a beautiful timber frame home on a thirty-one-acre farm. The home was set right in the middle of the parcel. It was extremely private and was exactly what we needed to decompress and relax away from the businesses. The property had a mountain view, amazing sunsets and was the perfect place to call home.

We both worked hard and enjoyed the home. We built a home office and had more than enough room to do everything we wanted and comfortably host our family. There was a large screened in porch where we would relax and eat dinner, enjoy the mountain views, and play board games like Rich Dad's Cash Flow with our nephews. It was a very busy time in our lives, as we were trying to settle in, run businesses, spend time with the kids, and still work our full-time jobs. I was also serving on the board of directors on several community boards at this time; a founding board of a local community dental clinic, a director at the local chamber of commerce, then promoted to Vice President, and even an eight-month stretch as the interim President, all the while my businesses were growing rapidly.

While I was running around like a chicken with its head cut off, giving 120% to my obligations, Meghan was managing the farm before and after work. We were raising chickens, turkeys and rabbits. We raised Thanksgiving turkeys for our family to enjoy and for Meghan's colleagues at the bank. We had created a nice little hobby farm and were really enjoying living the farm life. Our niece and nephews loved coming up and seeing all the animals we had accumulated, especially when hens went broody and we had little baby chicks running around. Add in a few sappy barn cats and two amazing dogs and it truly was an excellent experience for the kids.

We continued to get our niece and nephews on weekends and school vacations and instilled in them that anything is possible. We would do chores around the farm, play the Cash Flow game, dream big after dinner, and take a ride to our local favorite ice cream stand. At this time, we owned several real estate holding companies, a service company, and I was heavily involved in the community. Our nephews worked for us during the summers. They would live at our farm during the summers and the boys would work with me or my dad during the days developing the properties we owned. We had the boys pay their own way with their earned income and learn responsibility, hard work, and our family's high standards. They were able to see firsthand the fruits of our labor in the form of proceed checks. My business partner and I would bring them to closings, auctions, showings, business negotiations, and do our best to involve them in every part of the process. Although there were times they wanted to hangout after the work was done, they were understanding when we needed to spend some time in the office first. It was with great pride we were able to teach them these values. They would also listen to the audio books on self-improvement in the background of the truck as we bounced job site to job site, and back to the farm. It was a great bonding experience for all of us and formed some of our most favorite memories.

Meghan and I hit our major working together moment in 2015, when I bought out my business partner and became the sole owner of the two companies. Meghan became my chief of staff, my bookkeeper, worked with our CPA, and still found the time to maintain the farm and work full time at the bank. Jason and I had made our companies a pillar of the local business community, so to outsiders this separation was a new source of gossip. People talked, tried to influence us one way or another, or just tried to pry for information. But Jason and I were working through it. It was our first partnership, and we wanted to continue our friendship. There were still difficult decisions to make for the future of the business.

We had to wind down four years of partnership, our service company with its employees, and the holding company with all the real estate assets. While we had the wind down process in the operating agreement, we still had assets with cash flow and underdeveloped properties to consider. Meghan's experience was crucial in helping me transition and prepare the separation document for both of the entities. At the end of the tax year, I would assume sole ownership of the service company. It took almost another year to work through the holding company, with Meghan collecting rent and sending monthly reports to Jason during the winding down process.

This was a confusing time in my life. The stress and the uncertainty of the future often led to bouts of melancholy. Our routine was disrupted, we had to move offices, and we had to create new processes at a new location for the businesses. Luckily, I had Meghan to help me through the transition. But still during this time I suffered another blow to my morale. One of my best employees gave his notice. He and I had worked together for 8 years, and I relied on him to take care of properties and was planning on him helping me going forward.

Despite these events, the companies both continued to grow. Jason and I continued our friendship, planning yearly kayak trips and providing advice and support to each other. I'm proud of what we accomplished in the short amount of time we were partners. I learned not only to push through adversity, but to use it to keep up my momentum and drive my growth. Meghan and I both started learning how to work together in business and develop a routine and a process. We began to mastermind even more as a couple than we ever had based on everything going on. It wouldn't be until later that I'd see how this would lead to major successes in our lives. Our focus was to transfer more of our earned income into more real estate holding companies and assets.

At first, people thought we were crazy. They told us it was too complicated. Don't you already have enough companies? Why would you create more? We weren't going to let this stop us. Our careers had shown us how both sides of this worked, from being the banker to being the property manager and investor. It was finally time to put everything we learned to full use. It wasn't easy, doing things right never is, but we made sure that each company had entity structure, a mission, goals, and a succession plan. We ensured that our legacy was in place.

HOPE SHINES THROUGH LIFE'S CHALLENGES

A few years after we moved up to New Hampshire, we bought our first kayaks from an old storage barn on a pond. Meghan and I took the kayaks out on the pond for a test run, and I fell in love with the location. Over ten years later, as Meghan and I were starting our real estate empire, I saw that same barn for sale. I drove Meghan by it and I pitched my idea to turn it into a shop we could run our businesses out of. We decided what my spending limit would be and I made an offer. It was denied. I tried again six months later. Still denied. I often found myself sitting in the parking lot, adoring the property and visualizing myself there. It was the ideal shop and was only three minutes from our home. Easy commute. Months later, I tried one last time. Denied the third and final time.

Not too long afterwards, the property went to auction. I told my family about it. They told me I should go for it, Meghan agreed. With my two oldest nephews Jimmy and Michael working a job for my service company and Meghan at the bank, I took my youngest nephew Marcus and my mother-in-law as family support and good luck charms. I wasn't going to lose it this time. After a lengthy bidding war, I called Meghan to give her the news. This time, I was the winning bid and we soon relocated our shop!

Meghan was continuing to advance in her career at the bank during this time of personal growth. Meghan was promoted to Assistant Vice President Commercial Workout Officer. This position greatly expanded her reality and growth rate even further. It meant more exposure to entity structure, working more in depth with the bank's legal counsel, more new responsibilities, and more learning opportunities. She was handpicked to perform the due diligence on the acquisition of a pool of personal and commercial loans from another financial institution. Meghan showcased her risk mitigation skills as she assisted customers who were navigating tumultuous times in their business. She applies her underwriting, risk mitigation management, and commercial banking skills to our real estate companies, our clients, and collaborators. It's due to her vast knowledge of and expertise in commercial lending that we could achieve our success. I mean talk about knowing how to prepare your financials and provide the perfect pitch to your banker!

This was a major time for my family as well. Meghan and I were kayaking on a local pond, Rocky Bound, with our nephew and Meghan's mother. While we were boating, her mother had pointed out a property by the water and mentioned how nice it would be to have something like that in the family. Upon hearing this, we were inspired. It didn't take long for us to look into the property and do our due diligence. Once we had, we fell in love. It was a gorgeous house, and the price was too good to pass up. We decided to purchase it and have it become a major part of our legacy. Our niece and nephews would always have a place by the water they could come to relax or spend time with the family. For us, though we didn't know it yet, it would be our introduction to pond life.

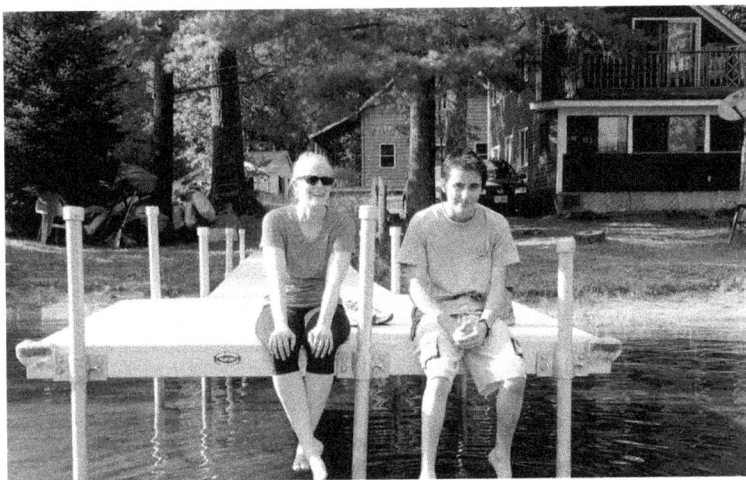

Meghan and Michael enjoying Pond Life

33

As we continued our growth at Cityscape, we entered niche areas of expertise in the real estate service industry. Our focus deepened within the REO and mortgage industry. My nephew Jimmy and I achieved licenses as EPA/HUD RRP Certified Lead Renovators. Jimmy's exceptional proficiency shined brightly when he aced the certification test with unmatched speed and precision, astonishing even the instructor. Our RRP certification stands as a testament to our dedication, and over a span of five years, CITYSCAPE LLC completed substantial lead abatement work within our community, which also greatly contributed to our real estate portfolio's development.

The undertakings were monumental in scale. A particular project demanded two years of exhaustive exterior and interior abatement. The Tyvek suits would come out, the respirators would go on, the containment would be set up, and the employees would start the job. Long hours in a suit, especially in hot or tight working environments, is a lot to ask of an employee. Regardless of how we felt while doing the work, it was always a great feeling to know that we helped these families and our community in such big ways. Following half a decade of involvement in the field, we opted to transition away from the lead abatement industry. The evolving regulations, high insurance costs, and endless paperwork eventually led us to this decision.

Around 2018, we decided to sell our farm home. It had appreciated well, our companies were taking off, and I was still continually working on jobs with my nephews. Our future was looking bright. The decision was prompted by a remodel on a water access cabin we had purchased for only fifty-four thousand dollars. While we were working on it, we had fallen in love with the lake lifestyle. We decided we wanted it to be more than a second home or rental. We also wanted to travel more and taking care of the farm made it hard to leave for any length of time. At this point we hadn't been able to take a vacation in years. The decision was difficult. It was our home, it was where we put down our beloved English Bulldog Joscelyn after thirteen years together, and it had become a gathering place for our family. Eventually, we decided to list the property and move on to experience what lake life had to offer. The house was sold to a TV celebrity from the Discovery show Northwoods Law, which was a great experience as fans of the show. Living there as long as we did, there were no capital gains on the sale of the home and we were free to move on to the lake. We decided to simplify things going forward with less expenses and more lake life while still serving our community.

STANDING STRONG AMIDST ADVERSITY

We settled into our new life well. Our expenses were drastically reduced and we gained more time not having to take care of the farm. The outbreak of COVID-19, however, had turned our smooth sailing into rough waters. Like many states, New Hampshire and Vermont had put moratoriums in place and banks were no longer able to foreclose on delinquent borrowers. The foreclosure industry ceased to exist in the blink of an eye. Our service company was faced with a severe setback. Our revenue suddenly dropped a few hundred thousand a year. Luckily, we had a variety of other construction work. Our twelve years in business was now a blessing and we were able to pivot. Unfortunately, the pandemic did cause us to have to lay off employees, which was a hit to my morale. Within the same span of time, an unexpected property line dispute materialized. It was another unexpected setback. Suddenly we had to hire a surveyor and engage a legal team. After an extended process, through unwavering persistence, our rights were solidified.

As if this cascade of challenges weren't enough, fate dealt yet another blow in the form of a rear-end collision. I was sitting at a red light and I was suddenly struck from behind. It happened so fast that the driver behind me totaled his work van. The accident had aggravated my prior back injury while also injuring my neck. After years of working through my medical issues and finally feeling better again, I felt worse than I ever had before. I could no longer do any heavy construction work. I was fortunate to have my nephew, Jimmy, to pick up the slack. He was experienced working with the family company and he kept our jobs going while I worked towards recovery. I didn't like putting that pressure on him. With the pandemic slowing down our income and me spending so much time at the doctor's office and rehabilitation, I was trying to search for the lesson in all of this. *Why was it all happening, and why was it all coming so quickly?*

Before answers could be unraveled, another heart-wrenching chapter unfolded. Our eighteen-year-old Hurricane Katrina rescue dog, Pinto Bean, had two vestibular syndrome episodes and he could not recover from them. It was traumatic seeing him go through it, each time we thought he was dying in front of us. Late one night, in the middle of a horrible snowstorm, Meghan and I drove over an hour to the closest emergency vet to end his suffering. The experience was heartbreaking. The circumstances were far from ideal, a sentiment that resonates with anyone who had to say goodbye to a cherished pet during the pandemic, as the once-comforting hospital experience transformed into something stark and sterile.

THE COMEBACK IS ALWAYS STRONGER THAN THE SETBACK

During these years, I was searching hard for answers while trying to get through the day to day of being a business owner. Holding things together is tougher than one thinks, especially after the hits we had taken. During this period of my life, I would listen to Napoleon Hill's 'Outwitting the Devil' over and over again, trying to keep my mindset on track and pull out the lessons, while everything else seemed to be falling apart. I was continually holding on to faith in Meghan's and my family's strength as we overcame this period in our lives. My adherence to principal was not only rewarded, but because of my conviction I was able to learn valuable lessons and have a renewed sense of spirituality. You just need to be willing to receive the positive message even during times of temporary defeat or setback.

The lessons I learned from these experiences shaped how I planned going forward. It also reinforced the principals we had been living our lives by, *It's not if, it's when.* By structuring our businesses with separate entities, proper insurance policies, professional vendors, and multiple income streams, we were able to overcome our hardships and preserve the legacy we worked so hard for. One of the seeds of greatness that came out of this time was the creation of Pond Life Vacation Rentals. It was born during this time of adversity in our lives. It was a way to keep busy and work toward the lifestyle we wanted. With some down time in the foreclosure industry, we buckled down and built a successful vacation rental management company providing high-quality vacation rental experiences to our guests. We had always built our companies to have reputations of their own, and by building on the good reputation of our other companies we were able to expand Pond Life rapidly. The cash flow it produced was able to provide for the free lifestyle we originally set out to live after selling the farm.

After navigating the challenges of the pandemic, the litigation, and other events over the past couple of years, Meghan made a significant life decision. She chose to depart from her W-2 job and instead assumed the role of CEO at Cityscape. Her successful career in banking and her strong commitment to running a top-notch real estate development company have been major assets for the company. Cityscape still specializes in providing property preservation, stabilization, and REO services to financial institutions, realtors, and investors. Expanding its offerings, Meghan introduced upscale cleaning services catering to vacation rental owners and clients in the Lake Sunapee region. I'm so proud to have her overseeing Cityscape.

Meghan's philanthropy is evident as she applies her extensive insights from her years in commercial banking into volunteering. Presently, she volunteers on the Board of Directors for a local non-profit credit union, a vital role where she leverages her knowledge. This credit union, serving the Vermont and New Hampshire communities, boasts assets totaling two hundred and forty-one million dollars. Similarly, I find honor in my role volunteering on the same credit union's supervisory committee. This cooperative financial institution serves a substantial membership of 18,000 across both states. I've also recently achieved the esteemed Certified Credit Union Supervisory Committee Member (CCUSC) Designation, recognized as the pinnacle within the industry.

It's a great feeling to have stood the test of time together, with over twenty-two years of having been together as of writing this chapter. Fast forward to now, we have turned into CS Companies, a family of specialized companies in the real estate industry. Our family of companies now owns and operates six real estate holding companies, each with their own organizational structure, framework and unique missions in the industry. Accompanying these holding firms are four service-oriented businesses, each entrenched in a different facet of the real estate sphere. Beyond our involvement in real estate holdings and small businesses, we also hold equity stakes in numerous start-ups. Our dedication to philanthropy remains unwavering, as we not only contribute through our corporate endeavors but also allocate our time to serve others.

Meghan and I uphold the most rigorous standards, where

integrity and honesty form the core of our values. We've also worked hard to press upon these very principles to our niece and nephews. Guiding them through the transformative shift in mindset necessary for a life of abundance proved to be quite a challenge. As engaged entrepreneurial professionals and business proprietors, we're well-acquainted with the demands this placed on our family dynamics. Being actively engaged in the community, collaborating with premier vendors and partners, and, to some extent, anticipating these elevated benchmarks within the family can undoubtedly create a unique set of pressures.

Creating a life of abundance and changing our mindset has allowed Meghan and I to live our life by design.

We are both under 40, as of writing this chapter, and were able to purchase a property in Florida and vacation there regularly. Critics told us we had to wait until we were older. "You have to wait until you're over 55 or retired at 65", they said. Well, there's no time like the present. Meghan and I have spent the last two years on the Beach for Christmas, as so-called snowbirds! It's been amazing and I wouldn't change a thing. Purchasing the property in Florida was a leap of faith. We knew of no vendors and didn't have a full plan, but we loved the area and we went for it. Sometimes in life if you spend too much time analyzing you will freeze up. As my accountant always says about my banker "What are they having analysis paralysis again? Let's get this deal done!"

OUR JOURNEY AS "HOSPITABLE HOSTS" INTO THE STR INDUSTRY TOGETHER

We wanted to give some more insight to "Pond Life". Meghan and I have always had a love for all things real estate, investing, and traveling, but I never knew how much I would end up enjoying the hospitality side of the portfolio. At a time when we were faced with great adversity in our lives, we decided to start a new venture in the short-term rental space.

As mentioned, we were already in the rental business for years providing long term residential housing and commercial rental space. We had an Airbnb account set up in 2018 for personal travel. One of our properties already had a furnished studio apartment we rented to traveling nurses for years and we had several waterfront and water access rentals. These properties seemed ideal for starting our first venture into this market. This decision started our journey to becoming hospitable hosts. We were blessed to have been hanging out at our water access camps for a few years at this point and we had a simple family saying called *Pond Life*. After a long day or long work week with the nephews it was let's go hang out at the camp and enjoy Pond Life. That simple family slogan has turned into far more than I could have ever imagined.

It was July, one of our favorite months, when Meghan and I founded Pond Life Vacation Rentals. Pond Life Vacation Rentals is a real estate vacation rental management company providing families access to all of New Hampshire's outdoor activities. Although we started the company right as the COVID-19 pandemic was ramping up and many had concerns about the strength of this part of the real estate industry, we continued to push forward with our vision. We were able to lean on our prior management and sound property management principles to guide us through this new endeavor. Often, we received words of caution from those that thought vacation rentals were nightmares to manage. We persevered through the trying times of the pandemic knowing that we have provided people from all walks of life with an opportunity to reconnect with nature and have access to water and outdoor environments. This was our *WHY* and we uphold these values to this day.

Pond Life Vacation Rentals has performed extremely well since its inception. We are finding that guests have rediscovered a desire to be with nature. Pond Life Vacation Rentals offers vacation rentals to all income levels and walks of life. We have had the honor to host top corporate CEOs, family, friends, world travelers, those looking to move to New Hampshire, and many more at our properties. It's a great feeling to be in the position to provide these guests with a peaceful sanctuary, either for their short-term vacation or temporary stay needs. We get to see and meet all kinds of people and they often share their stories about why they're traveling. Our guests trust us and we now have dozens of repeat guests. We are proud to have built a company reputation for creating memorable experiences for our guests to cherish for years to come.

Sunsetter Cabin

Pond Life Vacation Rentals has been an amazing experience for both Meghan and I on a personal level as well as a professional one. It was created out of a time of hardship in our lives and required us to pivot a bit, but our character, perseverance, family support, family slogan, and reputation drove us out of this temporary adversity and forward towards our mission. Even though we didn't know it at the time, the adversity planted a seed of greatness in our lives, a seed that blossomed even further when I was contacted by Jodie Stirling about becoming an author in a book called *Hospitable Hosts*. The personal call was amazing, and she was incredibly supportive of me joining the book. I was honored to be presented with the opportunity, especially after spending many nights listening to many of the hosts talk on Clubhouse. Oftentimes, I listen to audio books on self-improvement and developing a productive mindset. I did the same with Clubhouse, listening to and applying the advice the hosts were giving. I listened every Sunday like clockwork to Julie George's room and to the other authors with Meghan also lending an ear to the conversation. I am proud to be a part of the Hospitable Hosts book project and to know the other amazing authors involved in it. To anyone who has not picked up a copy, I would recommend buying it. It has crucial information for anyone interested in the STR and vacation rental industry available on Amazon, and I'm on chapter 25.

RETURNING GUEST REVIEWS

"We love it here! We'll continue to come back time and time again as the beauty is surreal! The hosts are awesome people! Thanks for a wonderful place to stay during our 4th of July weekend!"

—Jauntessa A. "The Little Cabin Retreat" Croydon, NH on July 4, 2022

"This was our second year staying here and everything was great as usual. Beautiful scenery, very relaxing. Pond Life Vacation Rentals were very responsive and accommodating. Looking forward to future stays"

—Cory M. "SunSetter Cabin" Croydon, NH July, 2023

Meghan and Andrew's Quick Tips to Excellence

We deeply appreciate your interest in this book, as it signifies your quest for invaluable industry insights and wisdom. While the limitations of a single chapter hinder us from recounting the entirety of our shared accomplishments, challenges, and transformative experiences, our intention remains unchanged. We've refined pivotal advice surrounding business insight, effective partnerships, and sound real estate principles. Through meticulous exploration of our life events, Meghan and I have carefully handpicked a collection of sturdy principles. These principles are meant to not only amplify your prosperity but also safeguard your well-being, spanning across both your professional and personal life.

Due Diligence: Our first tip to anyone who is thinking of buying a new property for an investment, is to take the time to do the due diligence and stick to the solid principle of *buy it right*. If you are an active investor like me, or someone who buys and operates a majority of their real estate assets, this will be crucial to your success.

When you ask any seasoned real estate investor, they'll say that you make money on the buy. The numbers have to work and you can't let your emotions do the buying for you. If you stick to this sound principle of buying an asset right for cashflow first, then that asset appreciates later on during your holding period due to market conditions and added value improvements, then that's all bonus! In the buy it right model, this includes your due diligence.

- Does it cash flow now?
- In the future?
- Is it a turn key property or does it need a cash injection to bring it up to your standards and life safety?

Don't be afraid to seek financing from a local bank or credit union. They may be able to offer an attractive rate and term, which will play into the buy it right model.

Proper Insurance: Our second tip would be to ensure you have the correct insurance policy. I have seen time and again where investors, business owners, and Airbnb hosts overlook such an important investment for their property or asset. Believe it or not, insurance is an investment and it's worth every penny. It covers and protects your assets and business operations. Make sure you are properly protected before going into any venture. I have found that being forthcoming about a rental property and amenities you will be offering at the property is vital to make sure that you are properly covered if something goes wrong.

Meghan and I once met with a couple that has been renting their second home on a lake. They were a great couple and looking to change their property manager and needed industry advice. After much discussion and several back-and-forth questions, I asked the couple if they had a proper short-term rental policy in place and if their insurance agent was aware they were renting the property weekly as a vacation home. With silence as their response, I could see in their eyes that they were not properly covered. To think they had a prior property manager that never suggested proper coverage was unconscionable. They were renting this property for years at weekly turnovers with huge exposure to risk and they never knew the danger. Although we did not end up taking on that account as a client, that day I was able to provide that couple with a referral to a local agent so they could obtain proper insurance coverage.

Also, do not overlook the importance of title insurance on your real estate property. It's an additional cost at the loan closing, but it's well worth the investment. Working at the bank, Meghan and her legal team put in claims against the title insurance companies on several occasions. I can say from personal experience it is a critical defense against litigation that results from property disputes or bad chain of titling.

Agreements: Our third tip is to make sure you have proper agreements in place. Having a proper rental agreement is following sound property management principles, which I highly recommend to any new investor, Airbnb host, or property manager who manages long or short-term rentals. We would also recommend that you have this rental agreement professionally reviewed by your legal counsel. Although some people are reluctant to add another initial expense, I cannot stress enough the value of proper legal counsel. We also recommend that you have your insurance company review and sign off on the rental agreements as well.

Nowadays, most insurance companies are requiring this process once they learn you are providing short-term rentals. There have been many times when an insurance company has strengthened my leases and provided stronger verbiage for the rental agreement at no personal cost.

I will mention that the arbitrage model has been very successful for some individuals going into STRs and backs up why I believe real estate is such a flexible vehicle for investors, but you still need to *lease it right* from the property owner. Following the advice above, it is good advice to make sure you have a strong mutually beneficial lease with the property owner you are leasing from. It is also important to align yourself with the property owner when it comes to the management of the property, otherwise you could be left hanging at midnight with zero support.

If you are operating from a business approach and have LLC's, Corporations, or Partnerships, having a signed legal binding agreement is crucial, even if you are a single member LLC. The operating agreements lay out the roles and duties of each member, director, etc. The same goes for vendor agreements. When choosing a vendor or contractor, first read their agreement carefully and be sure things are accurate. No matter what activity you are doing, signed agreements that lay out each party's responsibilities are important.

Cleaning: Another tip is understanding the difference between a short-term rental cleaner and a routine house cleaner. This is crucial for anyone who wants to make it in the hospitality industry. Guests have high standards when it comes to their short-term rental or vacation rentals and I have to agree with them as I expect the same when traveling and booking a stay. The last thing you want is a bad review when it comes to cleaning. No one wants to find hair in the shower or toilet or dust on the baseboard. Interview as many cleaners in your area as possible. Ask them to provide a checklist of what cleaning services they will perform at your property. Or better yet, provide a checklist to the cleaners of what you are expecting of them, and what your guests are expecting. Seeing a cleaner walk into a property with one spray bottle and nothing else is not a good sign. Top tier cleaning is just as important as guest communications. I speak to this as I understand the detail and care that is needed. I not only manage guests and cleaning operations for our companies, but I also support several STR owners in our area.

Communication and Honesty: When it comes to your marriage, make sure you are communicating with your partner. Meghan and I have such an honest relationship. We have seen what dishonesty and suspicion have done to close family members and we knew early in our relationship we were going to love each other differently. We may get annoyed with each other at times, but we have never gone to bed mad at each other.

We have a clear vision of our mission, both as a couple and

with our businesses. There have been many times where we have heard other people say don't tell her that, or the wife will never know. I'm not that kind of guy and she's not that kind of woman. We openly discuss all our experiences, good and bad.

The Reset Button: Breathe, reflect, and reset. Oftentimes, couples get to points where frustration builds up and emotions run high. The reset button is about pulling away from these situations. We take the time to breathe and calm down. We reflect on what's going on and how it makes us feel. Then we come back to the situation, having reset, and try a different approach. Doing this means we can communicate in a way that doesn't hurt the other and we don't have anything said in anger.

These three elements; communication, honesty & being able to reset, are the keys to success in marriage and business.

How Can We Achieve a State of Harmony with You?

Through our journey, we've learned that meaningful connections and dedicating ourselves to serving others are fundamental to achieving balance in harmony with the laws of nature. **Cityscape** has been in business for twelve-years. I am deeply grateful for the opportunity to collaborate with my family, collectively tending to the needs of our returning clientele. The journey of navigating various properties and projects alongside my family has been a tremendous experience. These memories form the bedrock of the *why* and the *how* within our family of companies.

We are always seeking opportunities to collaborate on deals and acquire real estate assets. Our experience and expertise allow us to react quickly to evaluate opportunities and potential management partnerships. Our full-service real estate development company can provide a broad range of services to our clients, including full remodeling, construction, property preservation and maintenance. For investors looking to purchase a property or sell their rental properties to investors in the marketplace, we provide consulting to help you obtain the best return on investment.

WWW.CITYSCAPENH.COM

TESTIMONIAL FROM A SHORT-TERM RENTAL CLEANING CLIENT

"We used Cityscape for the first time this year for our short-term rental turnover cleaning. I can't rave enough about their services: Every time the house was meticulously clean, and the crew always showed up and was on time by the minute. Meghan is simply a pleasure to work with. She is very responsive (even on weekends and holidays) and she thinks along the whole time trying to make life easy for her clients. Can't recommend their services enough if you have high standards and want peace of mind"

–Pascale- Vacation Rental Homeowner- Sunapee, NH

LETTER OF RECOMMENDATION FROM A CLIENT

"I write this letter of recommendation for Andrew Hanson CEO of CITYSCAPE LLC and his affiliates companies. I as well as my company have worked with Andrew and his company for more than 10 years. I have worked with Andrew in many capacities, as a real estate buyer, seller and most often a valued vendor. CITYSCAPE LLC has become my most valued foreclosure/REO service provider. CITYSCAPE has performed most any service I have needed for my REO properties, including, lock changes, cleanouts, repairs, all the way to a lead paint abatement. I have found CITYSCAPE to be responsive and professional and I could not ask for a better vendor to partner with on these properties.

Through the years of working with Andrew I have had a chance to get to know him as a person, I have found him to be an extremely hard working, motivated, professional person as well as business owner. This hard work and motivation have led Andrew to compile his own very impressive real estate portfolio spanning several area towns, both residential and commercial real estate. Andrew's experience with his own properties, as well as through his business is extensive and impressive. I would not hesitate to recommend his company as a top notch, well rounded real estate service company"

–Justin Ranney, Owner/Broker Coldwell Banker Homes Unlimited

CASH STREET TECHNOLOGY

Meghan and I are dedicated to providing exclusive coaching, business mentoring, and consulting services tailored to individuals who share our passion. If you're seeking professional guidance to excel in the real estate industry, we're here to support you every step of the way. By signing up for our couple's monthly mastermind or yearly couple's wealth and health retreats, you will get us as motivational mentors to help guide you through the business and real estate industry. At Cash Street Technology, we firmly believe that financial education serves as the backbone to solving many of the world's problems. Our goal is financial education through mentorship and collaboration with small business owners, real estate investors, property managers, and entrepreneurs to stress the importance of financial literacy. By investing time in one-on-one interactions with Meghan or I, you'll acquire profound insights and hands-on experience that will propel your entrepreneurial journey. We're committed to guiding you along the path to success.

Our pathway to achievement consists of **Four Key Pillars:**

- **Service Ventures & Small Businesses** – Including Trades, Boutiques, Restaurants – Cultivating Diverse Revenue Streams
- **Real Estate Portfolio Management** – Leveraging Tangible Assets for Steady Cash Flow, Equity Growth, Appreciation, and Tax Advantages
- **Intellectual Property Ventures** – Embracing Royalties, Patents, Licensing, Granting of Rights, Trademarks, and Copyrights
- **Philanthropic Endeavors** – Establishing Foundations, Active Participation in Local Boards, Community Engagement, Committee Involvement, and Voluntary Service to Empower Others Through Faith, Non-Faith and Shared Value Beliefs

WWW.CASHSTREETTECH.COM

MASTERMINDING WITH YOUR SPOUSE, FAMILY AND CLOSEST FRIENDS

This is the first time we have shared our favorite day of the week. Of all days, it's Wednesday! It's the middle of the week and we usually take off from what we are doing about mid-day, we call it "Wicked Wednesday" we grab the kayaks, go hang out on the boat, or maybe even take a walk together in nature at a state park. This is a time when we get to talk about our struggles, set goals, see where we can help each other out, or see if we are missing the mark on helping each other.

Although it has not always been our focus, we try to carve out time for ourselves and to make sure we spend time together once a week. As you can imagine, there are many times where life takes precedence and we must get something unexpected completed. The best part about our era is that your phone is a remote office if need be and the laptop usually isn't too far away either. But we have made a more concerted effort as our reality, business, and lifestyle grows to keep to our special day! It's always so peaceful on the pond, lakes, or trails we explore because everyone else is running the nine to five mantra and we are able to enjoy these areas pretty much all to ourselves. We truly enjoy this time to breathe, reflect, and reset.

A great quality of our relationship is that both Meghan and I accept change, allow our context to grow, and we don't follow the crowd. We are known to be trend setters! We have made our own way of life and we live it on our terms. It truly doesn't matter what your background is or the setbacks you face during your journey. If you hold onto your faith, you can make it through any temporary defeat or situation that life may throw at you.

We also mastermind with our family. Our nephew Jimmy makes it over just about every week for our family dinner. We not only mastermind on the real estate holding company he's involved in, we also talk about the family's lifestyle, upcoming goals, construction company's future, his personal workplace goals, and hold each other accountable for our progress. We also take this time to mastermind on the next family vacation. Who said that masterminding has to always be so serious? It's truly just the combination of multiple minds working towards a definite purpose. We even have a name for the three of us. We call ourselves the Trifecta! Three great people masterminding together as a family.

Meghan and I believe as you go through your journey in life, you will be met with many obstacles and problems. If you stay strong to your beliefs, be honest with yourself, and hold true to your character you will have the willingness to adapt, change, and solve those problems. Changing your reality or perspective will always lead you to find solutions.

Meghan and I would like to leave you with one last thought. As you hit transformative periods in your life, you must make sure to surround yourself with minds that think of abundance. You should also be aware you will be met in life with people who are naturally critics, bullies, cynics, disbelievers, pessimists, worriers, and many people that will just make assumptions without any facts. There will be many who will try to discourage you from your desires, visions, and dreams. Our advice is to stay the course even during times of temporary defeat and always find the positive or lesson in every situation.

Scan the QR code below to watch our interview on Youtube!

ACKNOWLEDGMENTS

From Andrew and Meghan Hanson

Our sincere thanks to the Authors of this publication. Your effort to help make this vision come true has been unparalleled. May it lead everyone involved to great achievements. Our sincere thanks for helping make our dream of this publication a reality!

To Bridget Sicsko, you have so many amazing talents! You are incredibly gifted and this publication would not have been possible without your unwavering support and commitment. Meghan and I are forever grateful and lucky to have your friendship.

To James Douglas, for your steadfast commitment to our family and company. Your editing is wonderful and we are beyond lucky to have you as our editor and part of our lives.

To our parents, for inspiring us to have big dreams and bigger ambition. Your love and support mean the world to us! We love you! With a special thanks to our nephews, niece and entire family, friends, and our tremendous vendors for their support of all our business endeavors.

Again, we are beyond thrilled to be part of this book and to share our story, especially since books have been a huge part of our success and mentorship over the years!

ABOUT THE AUTHORS:
Andrew & Meghan Hanson

Andrew and Meghan Hanson's journey began with humble origins, but their shared drive and determination have propelled them to become a formidable force in the business world. Andrew and Meghan are the dynamic duo behind multiple successful companies from real estate, small businesses to business coaching. Together, they have a strong background in financial management, entrepreneurship, and leadership skills. Those skills combined with their dedication to make a positive impact on the world, make them a valuable asset to any couple, individual or organization.

Andrew, a philanthropist and highly successful individual who achieved financial freedom and flexibility at a young age, which allowed him to focus on his passions. He is a best-selling author, having published works that offer valuable insights and strategies for success in various fields, including real estate investing, where he is an expert and has a wealth of knowledge, industry certifications, and experience. With a reputation for making smart and profitable investments, he is sought after as a personal business coach, helping individuals and organizations achieve their goals through his hands-on approach, infectious energy and visions. He is also an accomplished entrepreneur, having established and grown multiple successful ventures.

Meghan, a seasoned banking executive with over 16 years of experience in the industry, has a strong background in financial management and leadership. She is the founder of Pond Life Vacation Rentals and the CEO of Cityscape

LLC. Her comprehensive knowledge of backroom banking coupled with a highly analytical, collaborative, and strategic mindset help foster a forward trajectory. These attributes have been instrumental in her business achievements. Meghan's commitment to delivering exceptional client service is undeniable, and her dedication to facilitating client success is evident in all her endeavors. Her engagement as a Credit Union Board of Director further underscores her devotion to community enhancement and involvement.

Andrew and Meghan's unique combination of skills and experience provide a comprehensive perspective on how to generate value from all aspects of a business and distribute it throughout the organization. Their journey serves as a testament to the potential of two driven individuals coming together to make a lasting impact on their personal and business landscape and beyond.

Andrew and Meghan live in the great state of New Hampshire with their French Bulldog, Olina. Check us out at:

HTTPS://LINKTR.EE/MEGHANDOUGLASHANSON

HTTPS://LINKTR.EE/ANDREWHANSON

THE JOURNEY TOGETHER

BY STEVE AND CHRISTINE DUFFLEY

In the Beginning...Christine and I met in 1986 at the Joseph House where there was a weekly Catholic Charismatic prayer group for young adults. I had originally been invited by Fr. Marc Montminy to attend the group where Christine was already a part of the music ministry. Right away we had a few things in common. Not only were we both first born, a sure sign of independence, but we had both attended the University of New Hampshire, though interestingly enough, had not known each other during our time there.

While at UNH, my studies were in the construction trades and teaching, while Christine pursued a degree in social work. Since neither one of us was into the bar scene back then, it seemed quite natural for us to get to know each other through our prayer group community. Our very first date was a trip to Ben and Jerry's for ice cream which was located across the bridge from Christine's apartment. The four-mile walk gave us plenty of time to talk and get to know one another.

In the fall of 1987, after dating for one year, I knew I was ready to ask Christine to marry me. I really wanted to surprise her, so I had to get a little creative. I decided to do something bold, which was to sneak into an all Women's Cursillo retreat weekend and propose. After getting permission to do such a thing, I waited patiently in the chapel for Christine to come in after giving her talk that night. I knew that team members would routinely go to the chapel for prayer and a time of gratitude, and so I was confident she would be there. When Christine entered the chapel, she was shocked and quickly realized what was going to happen. From one knee I asked her "Will you marry me" and, without hesitation, she said "Yes." Her mom and Fr Marc came in and we received a blessing for our engagement. I still consider it to be one of the best decisions of my life.

Fast forward to a very hot August day in 1988, with no air-conditioning in the church, we stood before approximately 500 of our closest friends and family to commit our lives to one another in marriage. This budget wedding with cold cuts, kegs of beer and a very large homemade wedding cake served as a reminder that it was not the size of our wedding party, especially since we didn't have bridesmaids or groomsmen, or the reception that was going to make our marriage successful, it was the vows within the sacrament of marriage and the support of family and friends that would sustain us. Our wedding rings bear the inscription; *Colossians 3:12-17 (NAB)*. These verses are the practice of virtues and conclude with verse 17 that says, "And whatever you do, in word or in deed, do everything in the name of the Lord Jesus, giving thanks to God the Father through him." This reminder etched into our rings has created a foundation for us to build our marriage on through the years.

Today we have a beautiful picture that hangs in our living room, where our family gathers on a regular basis, that shows everyone at our wedding holding hands during the Our Father prayer. In fact, it was during the Our Father prayer as Christine and I stood together, that both of our fathers crossed the aisle and joined hands. Their action created a ripple effect and, before we knew it, the center aisle disappeared as each guest stepped out to join hands across the aisle. It was a beautiful moment that we will remember for a lifetime.

St Joseph Cathedral, The Our Father, 1988

BUILDING THE BUSINESS

As we embarked into our new life together, we both came into our marriage without any detailed plans or expectations other than our lives would be built upon our faith, mission and service. Christine recalls "I didn't know how many kids we might have or how much money we might make, but those things didn't really matter to me in the beginning years. In my heart of hearts, I simply wanted to serve others to the best of my ability, to serve and love God and to love and serve Steve as my husband."

For me, I don't remember being really concerned about the money as much as I was concerned about simply working hard to support us, and eventually our children. I knew that I wanted to be independent enough so that when our kids were older, I could attend their games and coach their sports teams along with other extracurricular activities. I knew that a typical nine to five job wouldn't necessarily make that kind of flexibility possible.

It was this early line of thinking that caused us to begin considering pursuing real estate as an investment and a means of income support. We realized that the entrepreneur lifestyle had the potential to give us the flexibility to take weekends when we desired to, to go camping with the kids or even spend a whole summer away.

However, it took us time to get to the point that we could make the leap to a more entrepreneurial work and lifestyle. Early on in our marriage Christine worked outside the home, as a station manager for WDER radio in Derry, New Hampshire. Meanwhile, I embarked on the self-employment route into construction work, which later would prove to be vital and extremely beneficial to our real estate journey.

However, my personal journey and early interest in real estate started because of my dad, Charles F. Duffley's Sr., and his work in the real estate industry while I was still a boy. In fact, dad operated the first real estate franchise in Manchester, New Hampshire called The Gallery of Homes. As a young boy of ten, I remember working in the real estate office, silk screening sales signs for properties and often helping my dad to clean out and fix up homes for sale. This early work eventually would lead to my own interest in real estate and discovering a gift for building and managing properties.

As a young man I started learning, through my dad, more about real estate investment, financing, the ins and outs of subdivision and permitting as well as funding. Dad purchased a beautiful three family Victorian house on East High Street in 1962 so that my grandparents would have a stable place to live. Moving in after college, dad and I partnered to work on the Victorian house to complete some necessary repairs and renovations. It was at this time that I got my feet wet, utilizing the rental rehab program to complete the work. Little did I know that this would be Christine and I's first home and real estate investment.

This first home on East High Street will always be a significant point in our life because it really marked our beginning as real estate investors. It is where we learned about rental agreements, managing income and expenses, and the art of people management. It was also a new way to look at living an entrepreneurial lifestyle and learning to understand that it came with both risk and freedom.

Following the East High purchase, we made a series of decisions based on market demand in the construction industry. The first of which was for Christine to quit her job at the radio station and become the president of our asbestos abatement company, Accurate Environmental Services. Yes, we were those people in the contaminant with white suits, respirators and gloves, crawling into tight spaces, and working in every basement imaginable.

The next two years were a blur as 1989 saw record high real estate prices. Christine would say we bought our first home, East High, the day before real estate prices began dropping. The recession officially began in 1990 but that did not deter us from exploring what might be our next investment.

In fact, we never stopped thinking about potential investments. Often, in the evenings after busy days, we would walk hand in hand, passing the boarded up, unsightly building around the corner that had burnt before we married. The smell of smoke still lingered in the air as we walked by. We would talk about how we would renovate it and fix it up.

Finally, when a *For Sale by Owner* sign appeared, we jumped at the opportunity. Wonderfully, the pieces fell into place with owner financing and funding for the rehab. To get the work done we utilized our asbestos work crews during down times and somehow made it through those twelve-hour days and just about seven days a week work shifts. We now had six tenants and two buildings with a storefront for an office. All was good and we were grateful for the opportunities we had been given.

Within the next year we also purchased a second building ravaged by fire for a mere twenty thousand dollars, only one mile from our house in the inner city. We reconfigured the six units to three by tearing down three of the units and making those into a parking lot. We then got approval to rebuild the other half into three, five-bedroom apartments, providing over twelve hundred square feet of living space in each unit. These were not easy projects but because of our determined vision, city officials were starting to take notice of our revitalization efforts.

Over time I learned how to close real estate deals and put together creative financing packages that worked with the more complicated HUD loan programs. This special funding allowed us to look for distressed properties and slowly build our portfolio. It also allowed us to begin restoring life to otherwise dilapidated properties and through our efforts, serve the people living in those neighborhoods.

The downturn of the real estate market that started in 1990 continued for years in our city. New England was hit hard during this period where investors and homeowners alike saw the real estate bubble burst. It was reported that some housing values dipped an average of thirty percent. Inner city landlords abandoned their properties or just did not care. Building after building became boarded up while foreclosure auctions filled two to four pages in our local newspaper. Several larger, iconic banks shuttered, with a total of seven New Hampshire banks forced to close and sold by the FDIC. We found ourselves in a very unique position to grow our portfolio in record speed through these auctions, paying pennies on the dollar.

From 1991 into 1992, we added four more buildings from auctions; twelve-, four-, six- and five-unit buildings. Each building was severely neglected and in the case of the twelve units, infested with cockroaches. Tenants that were squatting, and taking advantage of the bank takeover of the building, moved out quickly when we became the new owners, presenting them with Demand for Rents notices when rent was due.

We decided to start rehab on the twelve units first. I added greater value to the building by expanding and reconfiguring the units by converting the exterior porch to living area to livable spaces and enclosing the stairs. After calculating the cash upfront, adding a zero percent rehab loan and local financing, the numbers were strong. This single project proved to be our most profitable investment of time and money. Overall, this whole process continued to teach us the in-and-outs of bidding on foreclosed properties and utilizing HUD's funding through our local housing authority Rental Rehab Program.

As the economy continued to decline into the mid 1990's, we began experiencing a cash crunch along with changes in financing. It began when some of our newly remodeled units went vacant as there was an abundance of apartments on the market at very competitive prices. The lack of income created by vacancies and carrying costs of our last purchases, resulted in unpaid back taxes on one building, which in turn created a lien and blemish on our credit. Then, as if that was not enough, the remaining auction properties, once easy to get rehabilitation funding, were now subject to stricter HUD guidelines which now required one hundred percent lead paint removal, in turn escalating our costs and delaying our timelines. Refinancing after a cash purchase now became very difficult as some banks shuttered and others limited commercial loans.

For the first time in our marriage, we found ourselves barely making ends meet and calling creditors to arrange payments. We also had to shut down the asbestos part of our construction business because of changing asbestos EPA rules. Rules that stated it was better to manage asbestos in place rather than remove it entirely. This new ruling greatly lowered the demand for our services. Our workers, who crossed over between our asbestos and construction work, now had less work, resulting in layoffs. In truth, closing that part of our business was a real gut shot.

Yet despite the hardship, we worked hard to pay our bills on time and if we were going to be late, we made a phone call to help keep our accounts in good standing. Integrity in our business was important to us no matter the circumstances of the market or of our professional or personal finances. Treating others as we wished to be treated was part of showing that integrity, practicing the virtues we professed.

It was in this season that I found myself fighting depression over a three-year period. A big portion of what drove my depression was knowing that we could lose all our newly renovated properties that we had spent years of our life working and sacrificing for. I knew that we could possibly go bankrupt and deeply disappointed both our banks and private lenders. Adding to the stress were the difficult tenants we had inherited with our newest, but still rundown, properties. We had not been able to remodel due to funding difficulties and we were also dealing with a lot of maintenance issues. We considered ourselves "slum lords'" to those eleven units and it seemed as though there was no way out. We prayed, leaned on our community and just took one step at a time. A bright note that helped pierce that dark season was the birth of our first child, bringing us much joy.

One other positive thing was the invitation to work as a project manager for a non-profit that Christine and I both helped to start. My skill set in rental rehabilitation was an excellent match for the mission. During my time with them, the nonprofit did an impressive eight million dollars of inner-city rehab, reducing the number of blighted properties, tearing down large tenement housing, and building in its place owner occupied townhomes. It was a great feeling to be part of a whole neighborhood revitalization during that time.

The second positive thing that continued over those hard times was our relationship with our local St. Mary's Bank. From the beginning they always worked with us on our loan packages and treated us well, even during the difficult stretches. With diligence we were able to maintain a good credit score which allowed us to continue pursuing real estate once that long and difficult time was past us.

While those were tough years for Christine and I, we both just kept holding onto our faith that things would get better eventually. We spent a lot of time praying, (oh boy, did we pray) and we stayed active in our church. In fact, from our experience in the Cursillo movement from before we were married, we were now leaders in that space, with me helping to lead the men's retreat weekends and Christine helping to lead the women's retreat weekends. In fact, it seemed that Christine was pregnant in between every other retreat that was held. But as the years went by God always provided and in the process our faith continued to grow through the trials, as did our family, adding two beautiful daughters.

I left the nonprofit after three years. I used that experience to further our real estate and began to work in construction again, continuing to manage our real estate portfolio which numbered six buildings and over forty tenants. Today, my work as a commissioner on our local Housing Authority is a result of having that skill set in the nonprofit world and it allows me to give back to my community on an ongoing basis.

FAMILY LIFE

Stevie, Grace & Anne Marie were all born between 1992 and 1996; then in 2000 our fourth child, Luke, took over the baby of the family position. Honestly, we don't think Anne Marie ever recovered from the dethroning. Next to faith, family was the most important thing in our lives. I am the oldest of six while Christine has two younger brothers. It was also a huge blessing that most of my family lived close by allowing our kids to grow up with their cousins, while Christine's parents were only in the next town over.

With each new child born into our family, our love expanded. On one particular occasion Christine recalls the announcement and birth of the soon-to-be newest addition. "It was with great joy when we found out that my younger brother, Skip, was also expecting a child with his girlfriend. We all thought this was a positive sign since over the years he had experienced a lot of hard things in his life, including prison for a variety of offenses which included drugs. I really hoped that, with the birth of his son, my brother was turning the corner, but then the phone call came from my mom to tell us that Skip's son, Christopher, was born early. He was only 26 weeks gestation, weighing barely 1 pound and 12 ounces. I felt so helpless. Yet all we could do was pray because, as premature as Christopher was, there was no guarantee that he would live long. The uncertainty and the inability to do anything but pray drove me to my knees continually as I prayed for my brand-new nephew."

Thankfully Christopher made it through those early days of life but after three or four months we stopped hearing from Christine's brother. We knew that there must have been some kind of issue. It was during a weekend that I was leading a men's Cursillo retreat that Christine felt a tug on her heart. She felt God was leading her to find baby Christopher. When I came home exhausted that Sunday evening, Christine mustered up the courage to tell me what she had experienced and "was it ok" for her to call the state of Florida where she last knew Christopher's location. I agreed whole-heartedly and Christine made the call.

Christine was fortunate to locate someone in the Florida Department of Children and Families Services that knew who Christopher was and promised to call back with more information the next day. A return call was made and we finally had some answers. Christopher had been placed in a medical foster home because of medical conditions associated with his premature birth. We were told that Christopher had been exposed to drugs in the womb, testing positive specifically for cocaine at birth. In addition, parental rights were being terminated for ignoring court orders. However, the biggest shock was that Christopher was blind along with a litany of other medical issues. The voice on the other end of the line paused and then asked "Are you still interested?" Christine maternally said yes, and consulted with me to see what we should do. We decided Christine should go and meet Christopher and discern if we should take steps to gain custody of him.

Arriving by plane Christine called the foster home to let them know she had landed. However, somewhere in between the last phone call and the current one, we came to find out that Christopher had been hospitalized with double pneumonia. Instead of meeting him in the foster home, Christine met him in a hospital room, with no family by his side. It all seemed so sad, yet his spirit was so happy as he repeatedly bounced up and down in his baby bouncer, located in his steel crib, entertaining himself through motions and his own arm movements.

The nurses were fabulous and allowed Christine to hold and feed Christopher and to ask questions and be present as they cared for him. On the second day Christopher's very small IV came out of his foot and Christine recalls; "I remember watching as they tried to re-insert that tiny IV. Each time they tried, Christopher let out a scream, and each time, three in all, it pierced my heart. It was at this point that I began questioning, "How can I do this with four other children? Is it fair to them? Why am I even considering this?" Christine's questions, tears, fears and prayers were constant that entire week. Thankfully, Christopher became well enough to return to his foster home a few days later and Christine spent the rest of the week interacting with the family and other foster children. Yet, as her stay was ending, she knew we needed to be able to give the social worker an answer. "I remember getting down on the floor and pleading with God to show me what to do. With my face bent to the floor in utter surrender, I heard a little voice in my heart say, *Be not afraid!*

As I readied to leave, I called Steve and by the time our conversation was over, we were in agreement about bringing Christopher home. As we talked through our foundation, our calling and our faith we knew that we stood for life and we stood for family, and there was really no other answer other than yes."

It was at that moment that we said yes, a whole new journey opened up before our family. We made the choice to say yes in obedience to the message God had laid on Christine's heart and in doing so, I believe we experienced, and continue to experience, an amazing blessing in Christopher.

In *Mark 9:36-37* it says that when you receive a child in my name, you receive me. We know that every life is beautiful and we realize that if we are going to model that truth then we must be a family that stands for life and be willing to walk that out in a real, day to day way. Bringing Christopher home never felt like an obligation but more about being obedient to God's call on our lives, to live out our faith and to be willing to put family before everything else.

Christopher was fifteen months old by the time we were given custody of him by a Florida judge, allowing us to finally bring him home to New Hampshire. It was concerning that he did not sit up or even roll over when he arrived. The children, fighting over him like he was a new toy, were instrumental in his growth during this time, playing and encouraging him daily. Within months, Christopher began to improve and remarkably began to walk on his own.

Adding Christopher to the mix further made our first-floor

apartment a bit of a sardine can with seven people. We had attempted to buy a piece of land on the other side of town the year before, only to find out that the asking price was out of our reach. It was about three months after Christopher came to live with us that we received a call from the owner, who happened to be a priest friend of our family, with a counter offer that was very close to our original price. There was no need to contemplate the offer. We said "Sold!"

The pieces continued to fall into place and later that year, in November, we broke ground on our new home, the first single family residence our family had ever lived in. It was bittersweet to leave the only home our children had known, a home I had poured my talents into and the home we began our married life in. We officially moved in one year later with gratitude that our choices to be entrepreneurs gave us the flexibility to build and create an extraordinary experience for our children. We had just what we needed and an abundant life.

By the time we built our first home we had been married for fifteen years and had successfully been blending family and work along the way. Christine would manage the tenants and for a while, utilized her real estate license to help both buyers and sellers. However, life with a special needs child and four other children made for a very full plate so she deactivated her license as she moved to managing our family full time. She was the constant mom taxi van, bringing Christopher to therapies, school, and medical appointments as well driving our other four to soccer, basketball, clubs, play-dates, church obligations, and the regular things that come in the day-to-day life of a family. Thankfully, during those early years with Christopher, Christine's parents were a wonderful help to us. We are forever thankful for their unwavering support of our decision to raise and adopt him, always willing to care for him, find fun electronic toys at yard sales, and help with therapy appointments that were plentiful.

Overall, Christopher was a happy baby despite the total

blindness he lived with. As he grew, he began to exhibit behaviors that were very concerning. He wasn't communicating normally although he would say words. More often than not he would simply repeat whatever he heard over and over. When he was frustrated, he poked his eyes and banged his head on the floor. As he grew, he would withdraw into his own little world, struggling to converse with those around him. Testing would later reveal that Christopher lived with autism. At first, digesting and moving on from this news was difficult, but we knew who was in control, and it was not us! The first step was looking at the positive and embracing the beauty of his life, as we did with all of our children.

One of those positive things we noticed was that Christopher loved to clap his hands, keep a beat and experience any type of motion. In our home, we primarily played Christian music (and still do) so there was often a variety of Christian music that stayed on repeat. During that time Christopher really took to a song by Paul Baloche called *Open The Eyes of My Heart,* which later became a significant part of his personal story as he grew into a young man. To this day our children have a playlist on Spotify that holds all their favorite songs from those early years. As their parents, it has done our heart good to know that our children seem to appreciate the foundation that we gave them with those uplifting songs.

A FAMILY MISSION

Over the years we made continual choices to hold ourselves to a high standard, not only in our family but also in our business. We are sure we could have made a lot more money if we had chosen to operate our business by only looking at the bottom line, but we understood that our focus was much more as committed Christians. From the day we were married we have been on a journey to serve God to the best of our ability, to put each other first and be faithful in raising our children. Like any couple we have had our struggles as we worked to balance work and family. Often our family needed us, leaving little time for date nights or the ability to just have a quiet and decent conversation. Yet while it has not always been easy, living life with our family and working right alongside each other has been rewarding and filling. We realize, like many people do, that this life is not a sprint but rather a marathon that allows us to nurture our marriage, our family and our business.

In that nurturing, as we focused on our family and business, we worked to also keep our heart attuned to opportunities that would allow us to serve others outside our own immediate family. That day came when our neighbor and friend, Dave Rheault, mentioned to me that he was thinking about going to help a nonprofit organization called *Eight Days of Hope* and wondered what I thought about the opportunity. When I got home from talking with Dave that day, I proposed the idea to Christine, and without hesitation she immediately looked at me and said, "That's confirmation! We're going!"

Recently we had both been listening to the local Christian station and had heard them advertise the need for carpenters, and other skilled labor, to help families recover from Hurricane Katrina in the Bay St Louis, Mississippi, area. We knew that the skills we had developed through our rehabilitation projects and construction work would allow us to be a valuable asset to this rebuild effort. Plus, over the past year, we had made a little more money than usual in our business, and both had a deep desire to give back and tithe the extra income we had received.

That trip, the very first one, was December of 2005. We purchased an old RV that was sort of a clunker and beginning to rust. Christine did an amazing job of orchestrating five kids and keeping everyone sane during that twenty-four-hour trip to the Gulf Coast. We can thank the addition of a VHS, DVD player, and an assortment of activities that made everyone content

71

during the long drive. The kids were truly excited though none of us really knew what lay ahead, other than we were called and we were trusting God with the details. I vividly remember our last leg of the trip, traveling through long stretches of highway in the Mississippi fog. Christine was driving and I remember her tapping me on the shoulder. She said "I can't find a gas station" as she confessed that the gas gauge was now heading below empty at two-o'clock in the morning. With a quick prayer we pulled off at the next exit that promised a gas station, only to be disappointed to find it small and obviously closed. We resigned ourselves to sleeping near the pumps for fear of running out of gas but then I noticed that the pumps were on, so I tried my card. Bingo! The pumps worked and we continued down the road with our navigation system announcing the way. It was about 4 am when we finally pulled into the Christian youth camp that would be our base for the week. Christine eased the RV into the parking lot, turned off the ignition and we grabbed a few hours of sleep before our morning meeting with our first Eight Days of Hope group.

That morning we gathered to eat and participate in the morning meeting. Our group of seven stood out and we were affectionately called the "Partridge Family" by Steve Tybor, the leader. Our first job was to sheet-rock a tiny ranch home located in Waveland, one of the worst hit areas. As our family headed out in the RV, we began to see trees snapped like twigs, piles of debris, twisted metal signs, and cars in every imaginable position, scattered everywhere. It only got worse as we traveled further south with houses crumbed and badly damaged. We found our first home down a very narrow road and Miss Sissy, who was delighted to see us. Miss Sissy was in her late 70's, living in a FEMA trailer, right on her property. Steve got to work while we visited with Miss Sissy, listening to her stories in that little trailer as she constantly thanked us for coming.

At the end of the day, we knew that Miss Sissy was more

important than the physical work we were doing. Walking with people and giving them hope, was at the very core of this mission we had embarked on as a family; and if you ever need a shot of gratitude, just go to a place after a natural disaster and we promise it will change your life and perspective completely. Over all the years of serving, it has changed our lives in unmeasurable ways.

Today, Eight Days of Hope has become a far reaching, impactful organization staying true to its original mission; to be the hands and feet of Jesus, loving and serving those in need. To date Eight Days of Hope has now completed nineteen rebuilding events, and also aids in rapid response after a natural disaster. Most recently, in 2019, Eight Days of Hope also began building safe houses for survivors of human trafficking. I have been proud to serve as an ambassador for this organization since its inception. If you would like to know more, please visit WWW.EIGHTDAYSOFHOPE.ORG.

The Duffley Family with their RV at Eight Days of Hope 2005

OUR STR JOURNEY

Over the last few years, as we started doing some real estate planning, we began considering what we would need to do to be able to have enough cash flow so that we could step back to pursue our greater purpose and mission more fully; to love and serve others. While we both agree that we will never stop working as we get older, because we do enjoy taking care of our properties, we both agreed that we could do without some of the ongoing day to day work. So together, we began to envision what this legacy might do for our kids in the long run and also allow us to volunteer and be available to enjoy our future grandchildren. *What else could we do to maximize our cash flow that would allow us to start making a shift?* This was the point we started to consider short-term rentals.

Initially, we started to pursue short-term rentals because Christine really wanted a home in a warmer climate. We became even more motivated when some friends invited us to use their property in Cape Coral for a quick getaway. They had just completed their renovations, and we could see ourselves in Florida. If they could do it, we could too!

After a little research, we started looking for our first place in Florida. Initially we considered Cape Coral but then we started asking if there was any place available that would allow us to park our RV. Having just purchased a newer RV that we were using to travel to Eight Days of Hope events, we thought it would be helpful to have a place to store the RV when we came down to stay or do work on our rental.

Our realtor had a listing coming available the next day and we scheduled to be the very first ones to see it. It was a home located on the Fort Myers border, which included a beautiful RV garage with twelve-foot doors that was currently fitted with a car lift and hoist, certainly the envy of any mechanic around. It also included a beautiful pool, a three-car garage, three spacious bedrooms, and two full baths. It had the features we were looking for and we felt it would do well as our first short-term rental investment home. In fact, we found it so fast we did not have time to explore lenders. If we really wanted it, we had to move quickly. We offered full price, cash. Then we called up our favorite lender, Saint Mary's Bank and told them our plans. In weeks we had approval for cash. How do you ask?

By this time, our original twelve-unit apartment building, that we purchased when we first got married in 1991, had built up significant equity. Over the years, this Hall Street property has proven to be our income anchor and the best investment in our portfolio. The equity in Hall Street allowed us to purchase our first short-term rental property with cash.

It was amazing to us, that while it was a great leap, we didn't feel afraid of the jump. We saw it as an adventure and by this point in our business, both the construction and previous real estate properties had brought stronger financial security. We had unlocked a freedom we had worked hard for and it felt good!

We closed on the house and the work began. We knew the home needed to be attractive and have appealing amenities in order to get bookings (and lots of them) and make a profit. After some discussion, we agreed to hire a designer. Giving up control is hard for any DIY'er, but we thought it was necessary. The designer did a wonderful job allowing Christine to help find elements that matched the theme of the home, blending nature, practicality, and modern upgrades. I had the easy part of painting and addressing small maintenance issues.

Christine recalls coming in after all the renovations and design was finished and the new furniture was meticulously placed; "I cracked open the door, looking at the home as if I was the guest, and that's when it sank in, we own this! Wow, we did it!" We both felt so proud of how it had all come together and that this dream and goal of owning a short-term rental was now a reality.

Our next step was learning the ropes in order to rent to our first short term guest. Initially we started with a short-term property management company called Evolve. Their promise was that they would market our property, fill up the calendar and provide 24/7 support to our guests.

Even though we had a lot of concerns, and difficulty letting go again, we knew setting up a successful short-term rental was not something we knew a lot about. We decided to give it a go until we could figure it out for ourselves. We hired a local manager that also served as our cleaning company. The first guests came, then the second and third.

Knowing we could cash out and refinance Fort Myers, we began our search for a second property in Florida and stumbled onto an ugly, outdated property in a smaller town called Punta Gorda. Just as we found the property though, COVID hit the country. As a result, our initial lender backed out of the deal and we had to get creative to save it. One solution was a bridge loan, using the Fort Myers house. While costly, this financing move saved the deal. You might ask, was it worth it? Once we remodeled the Punta Gorda property the equity increased, as did the value of homes in that area. It was a good move by taking the worst home on the street and turning it into a beautiful, desirable property to either rent or resell.

Today, this home has two full bedrooms with three bathrooms, plus an entire upstairs with three additional beds, a pool table, and another set of couches. With the skills Christine learned from our first designer, she was able to bring a really nice touch to this home, sourcing most items from Habitat for Humanity, Home Goods and Amazon.

What has been so rewarding about embarking into short-term rentals is that it brings together our own unique skill sets to the project and creates adventure in our marriage. In fact, we have been able to include our children in the process as we tackled each property. Oftentimes they helped with repairs, cleaning, marketing or decorating. Christopher in fact, now at the age of 22, is very tech savvy and often will come down and help us with those elements for our properties.

Our son Luke also came on board with us full time as Punta

Gorda was being transformed. He set up our listings, helped with communicating with our guests and along with us, kept learning best practices, how to get things booked as well as serve our guests as best as possible. We were then able to cancel Evolve and began managing all our reservations ourselves.

As we continued to pursue short-term rental opportunities in Florida, we realized that it might be a good idea to seek out others who were pursuing similar goals. It would give us the opportunity to grow in our knowledge, bring more light to our bigger why in this space, tap into expertise, and have accountability, especially as we pursued some key financial goals and legacy planning. I attended one conference to learn more about the short-term rental market, and while I didn't find the conference overly helpful, the value was in the people I met that weekend and who I still stay in touch with today. Then I met Bill Faeth.

Bill began *Build Short Term Rental Wealth* as a way to fill a gap in the market for information on owning and running short-term rentals as he too, like many of us, was pivoting during COVID. I found a lot of value in his free content and engaged with him and others on his online Facebook group. Then one day I got an email from him. He personally invited me to become a founding member of the Build Short Term Rental Wealth Mastermind. He was hand picking a diverse group of people who shared a passion and a variety of skills in the short-term rental space.

After an hour phone call with him, I joined and Christine was added after realizing we needed to do this together. While joining the Build Short Term Rental Wealth mastermind has come with a financial investment, we have met some amazing people that have so many similarities to us, allowing us to grow together, as a group, as a couple, and individually too.

The first meeting of the mastermind was in April of 2021 in Gulf Shores, Alabama. Neither one of us had been to that area.

What exactly is Gulf Shores? Well, we found out pretty quickly that it was one of the top vacation markets that resulted in a strong return on your investment. This piqued our interest and Christine started to get curious, looking at properties during our time there while we were attending the mastermind meeting.

Our time at the meeting encompassed examining our *why* and retirement plans, meeting local bankers and hearing from an expert local realtor. Shortly after our weekend together in Gulf Shores, Bill had put a beach property under contract. Funny enough, Christine had looked at that same house online and thought it had a lot of potential. Long story short, Bill decided that it was just not the right fit for him because of the work it entailed. Steve had told him we'd be interested if he didn't want it. Fortunately for us, the owners agreed to allow us to take over the contract as long as we could close by the same date.

It all seemed to line up. We needed to move fast because there were backup offers and nothing on the market at that point. We made a quick decision based on its location directly on the beach and its configuration; three king sized beds, three full baths, and one bunk room. Additionally, the banker from First Cahawba Bank that we had met earlier got us approved quickly, in particular because Christine was able to get our financials together in record time. The other thing that influenced our financing was the fact that we had the sale of one of our New Hampshire properties ready for a 1031; where you are able to defer both state and federal capital gains, by selling an investment property and replacing it with a *like kind* property within the guidelines set forth by the IRS. This carry over of equity which served as our down payment on the $950,000 purchase price, was key. We closed on time and now owned a home directly on the Gulf of Mexico, with its own beautiful, awe-inspiring view on the beach. We named it, *Blue Angel*, after the Navy's Blue Angel fighter planes who now travel promoting Naval aviation and our nation's service members.

Once the sale was completed, we quickly made some key changes to the house such as new grills, bedding, and beach gear. We also deep cleaned the property, fixed what we could, and then opened up for bookings. Honestly, we couldn't have been prouder to see this property fly and yet, with anything, there came an immediate challenge. No less than twenty-four hours after our first guest checked in, the power started going in and out. Thankfully our guests were past renters of this home and were so very gracious as we worked to find an electrician who could take care of the problem. While our guest took the day out, the electrician managed to change out the house main electrical panel and the interior fuse box. While not something we wanted to encounter right away, when you manage properties, these things are bound to happen. Thankfully, once 2021 ended we were in the black enough to pursue the renovations on this property that we had hoped to start that spring.

Amy, a guest, left this review following her stay at the newly renovated Blue Angel house:

"This was one of the best family vacations we've ever had. The setting was ideal for a family—so easy to get back and forth to the beach—and the house was roomy, clean, comfortable, and had everything we needed. It was incredibly quiet and you can't beat the views. Highly recommend it."

Although this opportunity had a lot of moving parts, we look back and conclude that it fit perfectly. The property is on track to perform well year after year and it matches our desire to serve because it's just not about the building, but more importantly, the guests.

When Christine calls each incoming guest, she tells them our goal is to provide a memorable, stress-free vacation. This is our mission with all of our rentals, whether it be large or small like one of our newest homes called The Cozy Cottage. This seven hundred square foot home found its way into our portfolio when other options fell through during our second 1031 exchange sale. The Cozy Cottage was literally the last one on our notification notice. We were not happy with the price but we knew it was our last chance to keep the proceeds from the sale of East High to our son Luke from going into Uncle Sam's pocket.

Surprisingly, The Cozy Cottage stays booked continually because it meets a guest avatar that is not being met in that area and is situated near the beach, not on the beach. Its location makes it affordable compared to the larger homes, it sleeps five, and we accept non-shedding dogs. With its recent renovations in 2023, this investment is on track to produce double the income of the property we sold it for, which in turn, was part of our plan.

Currently, we now hold five short-term rentals and three long-term properties with nineteen tenant households plus our personal home. We look to the future with the possibility of moving equity from two more buildings into better income producing opportunities. Weekly, Christine and I set aside time to strengthen our why, refine our financial statements, and consult our fellow investors in our professional short-term rental circle and mastermind.

COUPLE TIPS - STR TIP - MASTERMIND TIP

The greatest catalyst for any couple looking to invest in short term rentals is really knowing your *why*. Our overarching reason for pursuing short-term rentals is to create financial income through meaningful work that allows us to serve on mission, pursue our faith, have time with our family and have the ability to leave a financial legacy and generational wealth. We have agreed, this is what drives us.

Just as important as jointly knowing your why is the ability to work with all kinds of people, from contractors to guests. If you are not a people person, it will be a struggle to fully maximize and enjoy your investment. If you are strictly looking at short-term rentals as a return on your investment, and do not really want to work directly with people, then consider hiring a property management company you can be proud of.

Whether you are on the front, middle, or back management, understanding, empathizing, coordinating and interacting with people is vital to success.

The reality of self-management, that allows for maximum profit, is that you will have bad days, challenging days, and things will happen that do not make sense. It is on those days, that you can go back to your why and remember the reasons you made the choice to invest in short term rentals or perhaps in any type of real estate.

Just like any other venture, you will want to evaluate your current skill set as a couple before jumping into short-term rentals. As we shared throughout this chapter, my skill set in construction has served us well as we have purchased and rehabbed various properties. For us we enjoy rehabbing, redesigning, re-purposing, and integrating our skill sets into our short-term rentals. We know that as we do this work, we are providing a great service to people coming into our properties.

A great way to continue evaluating your investment is to take the opportunity to actually stay in your own properties. We often stay at our properties to deep clean and perform vital maintenance such as filter cleaning, paint touch ups, restocking amenities, and any issue that may have arisen in the previous weeks. Staying overnight also provides the feel of bad weather, testing of appliances, placement of items, and things we would not ordinarily notice if we had not spent time in the home. An added benefit is that we make it a point to reserve one week at the beach with our family, bringing a "checklist of to-dos." It allows us to come together as a family to work, and enjoy our home, creating our own memories.

The final tip, in regards to launching into short-term rentals, is the importance of knowing your financial status prior to diving in. By understanding what resources you have available then you will be able to properly evaluate properties that come on your radar. Christine has done a great job in keeping our financials up-to-date so when we need to approach a lender everything is accurate and ready to go. Knowing your financial numbers also helps you know when things are not going well or a property is not bringing in what it should. Knowing your numbers, both good and bad, allows you to make appropriate and critical decisions about your investment and your motivation.

On a more personal front, it's also important that you don't lose your sense of humor and never take yourself too seriously. And when working with your spouse it's vital to intertwine forgiveness and mutual respect for one another in the day-to-day work of the business. Christine and I often reflect back to that hot August day almost thirty-five years ago, when we stood in front of friends and family, and made a promise to be committed to one another. No matter what life has thrown our way, through all our family and business journey, one thing remains, and that is our commitment to one another and the foundational principles we have built our life on.

MASTERMINDING AS A COUPLE

We both started out in separate masterminds, men's and women's, many years ago for personal growth. Deciding to join a mastermind together came about when we were seeking to maximize and diversify our real estate investments. As we ventured into short term rentals, we realized how much there was to learn. Instead of struggling and making costly mistakes, our decision to join a short-term rental mastermind connected us not only with other investors, but people with a variety of talents and resources. For example, our strongest skill is construction and rehabilitation while another member is accounting, another marketing, and the list goes on. What was particularly helpful was attending an additional couple's mastermind retreat, where we took the time to be challenged with priorities, goals and specific action items. We would not have accelerated so quickly, and with so much confidence if it weren't for the investment in the retreats, friendships, and defining the steps toward our retirement goals as a couple.

WHAT IS YOUR NEXT STEP?

In giving a call to action we cannot belabor the point that it is important that you know your why. Knowing your why sets you up for more realistic goals and the success of them. Some questions to consider:

- What is your motivation to explore real estate or short-term rentals?
- What are your overall 5-, 10-, or 15-year goals?
- How does owning an additional home impact your financials, time, and skillset?
- How will it impact your marriage, family, or relationship?

These questions, and more, will help you discover feasibility and help to build unity going forward. We suggest answering each question separately, then coming back together to discuss. For further discussion consider:

- If this building were to burn or become a victim of a natural disaster, would our lifestyle or standard of living be affected?

◆ How would our relationship thrive under this or any stressful event that may occur during our ownership?

Dig deep and save yourself some disappointments. Having had one property burn and two go through Hurricane Ian, we can testify to the patience, organization, mindset, and flexibility, among other things, you will need to handle such events. If, after considering these questions seriously, you are still nodding your head yes, then continue to find others in the industry you can trust.

Join Facebook groups, read books like this one, listen to podcasts together and begin to build your plan and then your team. Pursue being a lifelong learner in this ever-changing industry. COVID is just one example of how quickly things can change.

As mentioned prior, consider joining a Mastermind of other like-minded individuals that can push and challenge you beyond your own mindsets and comfort zone. When the unexpected happens, these fellow investors will be your advisors, and even lifeline, as you navigate your next decision.

Personally, our recent action item is focused on legacy, with both of us in our sixties. It is exciting to look back and know we have created a portfolio that gives us the freedom to do the things we have been talking about for a long time, one being our goal of building generational wealth that goes beyond just the material parts of our lives. We truly want to leave a legacy of wealth for our children and their children, that embodies a love for God, a love for one another and a love for serving others. That kind of investment, into the lives of others, will always far outweigh any financial benefit we receive from all our real estate holdings.

That has never shown up truer in our lives than through the life of our adopted son, Christopher. Remember that he was a little boy born at just one pound and twelve ounces with cocaine in his system, fully blind, and with a multitude of other health challenges. Today, Christopher, despite his earlier years of struggling to communicate, is now a gifted singer, musician, speaker, and above all, a technical wizard in the accessibility world of blind people. When he was elementary age, we discovered with music therapy that he had a special gift of perfect pitch. He had always loved music so we used his strength of music to build on his communication and love for life. Word of his ability to sing got around after he sang the national anthem first for local events and then for the Boston Red Sox. It wasn't just the anthem he loved; he loved Christian music. Knowing this, a friend of mine invited me to share a piece of Christopher's story which then culminated in Christopher singing his very favorite song by Paul Baloche, *Open The Eyes of My Heart*. The video of myself telling our story, and then Christopher singing, was then shared on YouTube and went viral, which has since impacted millions of people all over the world, giving them hope. Since then, Christopher has had the amazing opportunity to impact others through his singing and speeches for national events, galas, schools and a variety of conferences across the United States.

The reality of Christopher's story and the intersection of our lives together, would never have happened if we had only focused on spreadsheets and profit in our early years. However, because our larger why was first and foremost to serve on mission, despite the personal cost, it allowed us to say yes to Christopher. It also allowed us to say yes to our other four children as well as the lessons that we were able to teach and model over the years. In fact, we recently sat down with them to ask them how their lives have been impacted by our choice to be real estate entrepreneurs.

Some of the things they shared with us had to do with our family time together; staying at the lake, having their parents available to coach, volunteer, and attend their school outings. They recalled what it meant to see us as a model of freedom of choice, which then enabled them to become the best versions of themselves without our preconceived notions. They talked about what they had learned about the trades, the art of managing people, and how they are now learning to acquire their own properties. One other moving thing is that they learned the value of sacrifice and how important serving our tenants and guests were, that we were different and putting people first was the right thing to do.

They also shared memories of difficult situations that taught resilience, such as a sudden storm taking down trees and damaging the roof of one of our largest buildings. They were witness to the stress and worry of tenant issues and finance but also witness to learning how to problem solve and handle conflicts of all sorts. Overall, they beamed with pride though, knowing that someday, all the hard work, sacrifice, and planning would come to them. They knew we had made a plan and we wished for them to share in our mission to serve others and put family first; and that this income, that they will inherit one day, will continue to produce abundance in their lives and in the lives of others.

As we draw this chapter to a close, we look back on our story and see how from the beginning of our marriage to now, God has brought it all full circle. Faith, mission, and service, continues to be the call of our lives and that of our family today. Thank you for joining us in our journey this far. We are so grateful for each of you who have read our story. As we have done with other couples seeking advice, we invite you to connect with us at the link below. There you can follow our journey and tap into resources that will be invaluable to you as you decide your next steps. Yes, you can take action **NOW!**

You can visit us at **WWW.STRCOUPLE.COM** . Until then, may what you do, not only create wealth, but everlasting value to all whom you serve.

Passing on the legacy, Luke Duffley, pictured with Christine and Steve, closes on the family home on East High Street, Manchester, NH

Scan the QR below to watch our interview on Youtube!

ACKNOWLEDGMENTS

From Steve and Christine Duffley

First and foremost, we extend our deepest gratitude to you, the reader, for picking up this book and being curious about our story. Over the course of the last thirty-five years of marriage, business ventures, and countless moments of abundance, we have ridden the roller coaster of life's adventures, relationships, and emotions. What we have discovered is that living a truly abundant life demands courage and a steadfast commitment to one's deepest calling.

While it is impossible to individually acknowledge each person who has influenced our lives, if our paths have crossed, we thank you for being part of our life's fabric. We are also grateful for the opportunity to share our story with the other couple authors in this book and the trust placed in us by Meghan and Andrew. We are honored to be their friends.

Victoria Mininger, and the publishing team, we wouldn't have made it to the finish line without you, many thanks!

Thank you to our parents that gave us roots, wings, and for being our first teachers of life and faith and to our children, who now as adults, have confirmed we are not crazy but did "a good job" raising them. You are our greatest investment, joy and blessing.

Most importantly, our lives would not have experienced the abundance of blessings without a loving God, who gave us Jesus to show us how to live and love one another. In John 10:10 we are reminded "I came that you may have life and have it abundantly." With grateful hearts we humbly share our story, hoping and praying we might inspire your journey in some small way.

ABOUT THE AUTHORS:
Steve & Christine Duffley

Christine and Steve Duffley are a dynamic couple with a passion for real estate, business, and creating a life of abundance. As founders of Duffley Development Corp, their journey has evolved from residential and commercial construction to becoming masonry repair experts. Over the course of 35 years, they have also created a diverse real estate portfolio of both long- and short-term rentals.

Both are alumni of the University of New Hampshire, with Steve specializing in building trades and Christine in social work. With an impressive four decades of construction experience, Steve brings exceptional craftsmanship and problem-solving skills to every project he undertakes. His accomplishments range from new builds to the complete renovation of fire-damaged structures, as well as the reconfiguration of homes and apartment buildings for enhanced functionality. Complementing Steve's expertise, Christine assumes the vital role of financial management and tenant relations. Her dedication to money matters and fostering positive relationships with tenants and guests adds a crucial dimension to their shared success.

Beyond their professional endeavors in real estate, Christine and Steve are deeply committed to their local community and Catholic faith. Steve has served on the St Mary's Bank Credit Union board, acts as Chairman of the Sarto Center Retreat Center Board, and remains actively involved in the New Hampshire Cursillo Moment. Christine, on the other hand, is the President and Founder of The FIRE Foundation of New Hampshire which supports special needs education in NH Catholic schools.

Following the devastation caused by Hurricane Katrina in 2005, Christine, Steve, and their young family began their volunteer journey with Eight Days of Hope, a Christian non-profit organization that aids people in rebuilding their homes after a natural disaster. Steve has attended all 19 rebuilds and continues to serve as an ambassador for the organization, which has grown substantially over the years.

However, their most profound joy and investment lie within their five children. Notably, their decision to adopt a special needs son named Christopher has unexpectedly impacted countless lives around the globe. A YouTube video featuring Christopher's heartfelt singing, accompanied by Steve sharing their story, has garnered over 60 million views instilling hope in people's lives. All five children actively participate in their real estate ventures and have grown into successful adults. As a family, they witness the beauty of life and importance of family.

Driven by their passion for real estate, entrepreneur lifestyle, dedication to community service, faith, and unwavering commitment to family, Christine and Steve Duffley serve as an inspiring example of what can be achieved when passion and purpose intersect. They have proudly shared their journey on podcasts, radio, TV and print media.

HTTPS://LINKTR.EE/DUFFLEY

THE SHAE & RYAN STORY

BY SHAE AND RYAN DUFFY

Spring 2005, we met by chance on the white sands of the Gulf Coast. Shae, 18 years old, was on Spring Break her senior year of high school with a group of friends. Ryan was stationed at Fort Polk, Louisiana and 19 years old.

Just a chance encounter and a series of events led us to be at the same beach at the same time on March 26, 2005. Looking back, we certainly met with fate. We both seized the opportunity at true love and dove in head first. Just three months after Shae graduated high school in Xenia, Ohio; we were living together at Ryan's parents' house in the suburbs of Chicago. From the very beginning, we were leaping into high-risk situations and thriving in chaos. People looked at us like we were crazy but we were both never so sure about anything in our lives.

Our story begins in what is now a thriving STR market that we hope to invest in one day: Panama City Beach, Florida.

MAGIC WORDS: *SPRING BREAK*

Ryan: It was late March and we were just informed that we were relieved from duty for four full days. My friends and I decided to load up our cars and head to Florida for a few days to partake in some Spring Break activities.

We put virtually no planning into the trip. When we pulled into town on the night of March 25th, 2005 and there were no hotel rooms available. The earliest we could check into a room was the next afternoon. So, we did what I think any other logical person would do in that situation (as a nineteen year old), we spent all night exploring the town and ended up digging out foxholes on the beach to sleep in.

It ended up being a late night. The next morning, or quite possibly early afternoon, as we were waking up from our sandy naps, I was embarrassed to hear one of my colleagues calling out (or hollering) to a group of girls walking down the beach. One of the girls decided to give my buddy a chance and began heading in our direction. For that I will be forever grateful.

Shae was one of the girls in that group and felt compelled to follow her friend as she approached this odd group of people sleeping on the beach. Over the next few hours we didn't speak much, but found ourselves magnetically catching each other's gaze.

We played volleyball. On opposing sides. I'm pretty sure my team dominated hers, but honestly, I don't remember. She was beautiful and way out of my league. It was all a blur. After the game, we all started walking to the water to wash the sand off ourselves. As we approached the surf, I found myself walking alongside her. I didn't know what to say. I was nervous. I was scared. Without thinking, I reached over and picked her up (we hadn't even had a conversation yet!) and carried her into the water with me. I fell in love with her before we ever spoke.

Yes, I know that sounds weird but you really would have to have been in the moment to appreciate it. There was this unspoken connection that to this day I still can't adequately describe or quantify.

Sunshine and Rainbows

We had an amazing time growing up together as very young adults. Shae insisted she be twenty-one at our wedding so we had, what felt like, a long engagement. Shae began putting herself through college just one year after we moved in together and Ryan worked at various jobs, still figuring out what he wanted to do. We both always worked, mostly in the food industry. Shae was a waitress while attending community college and Ryan was in restaurant management.

Shae decided to major in interior design and enrolled in a prestigious school in Chicago. Ryan was very fortunate to land a job at the Chicago Fire Department. The waiting list is years long and he got on just a year after taking the test. We moved from the suburbs to the city and really had a blast. The food, comedy clubs, blues, festivals, and so many things Chicago had to offer we experienced. We also managed to travel some (sure is easier before kids!). We are both bold and are always dreaming up the next big adventure. We still had our struggles here and there. Money was always hit or miss and neither of us had impressive jobs prior to marriage.

Ryan: Within days of getting married, I was starting the Chicago Fire Academy. This was a job that kids dream about. A job that people make movies and TV shows about. A job that has a great pension plan. The type of job you never quit. Being a fireman quickly became ingrained as part of my identity. I loved it. I loved the rush and the camaraderie.

The schedule seemed too good to be true. We worked twenty-four-hour shifts with forty-eight off in between and every fifth shift was our day off. It comes out to about eight days a month. Of course, those eight days per month are FULL days. If the bell rings all night long, you're not getting any sleep. I was twenty-three years old though. It wouldn't phase me a bit. The thought of having so much open time in my schedule was incredible.

Having all of this new found time in between shifts, the logical thing for me to do (with the mindset I had then) was to take on more work. Shae was still working her way through her Bachelor's Degree at the time. The student loan debt was starting to rack up pretty quickly and we were eager to get in a position where we could buy our first house and start living the American Dream.

So, we started settling into our new routine. I would work my shift at the firehouse and come home for a little sleep. Then I'd be off to my side job for the next couple of nights. Shae and I wouldn't see much of each other but it wouldn't last forever. We felt like we were doing what we had to do to achieve our goals

I looked forward to my shifts at the firehouse. The first year on the job you're considered a candidate firefighter. In reality, you're the candidate at your house until a new candidate comes in on your shift. The low man on the totem pole has to earn his spot on the couch in the TV room. You're the first one in at the start of your shift and the last one to get relieved the next morning. The candidate is expected to work the hardest at a fire and learn from the veterans who have earned their seniority. I was honored to be a part of the organization.

Roughly six months into the job, we get called in as the second truck at a working fire in a three-story flat. I was assigned to a truck company. The truck's role primarily is to conduct search and rescue operations and mechanical ventilation (busting windows and cutting holes in the roof as the engine company puts water on the fire). This releases heat and smoke from the structure to help improve visibility and living conditions while the fire is being put down. Once the fire is under control, the trucks move on to what they call overhaul. You rip away the ceilings and walls in certain areas to make sure you don't still have some fire smoldering away in a void space that might rekindle later.

The fire originated on one of the lower-level units of the flat. It was an old balloon framed building, meaning there were minimal fire breaks running along the exterior walls from the first to the third floors. The thermal imaging cameras (TIC) were picking up little hot spots all over the place that we were trying to chase down. We spent the next hour or so pulling the ceiling and making holes in walls trying to get water on them. At one point we come to the kitchen in one of the apartments and the TIC spots something in the wall behind the refrigerator. Not normally that big of a deal but there happened to be a big hole in the floor in front of this fridge where someone likely cut access for one of the engine companies to spray water down onto the fire below.

This was a job for the candidate! I jumped in and straddled the hole to grab onto the refrigerator and pull it away from the wall. There was no way to pull it out without dropping it into the hole, but luckily there was a large window on the wall next to me leading out to the porch. The plan was to pull the refrigerator out just far enough to turn and push it out the window. With an awkward twisting motion while balancing over a hole in the floor, I picked up that fridge and manhandled it out the window. I felt a pop and a quick shot of pain down my right leg.

The adrenaline from the fire was still running pretty high and I was the new guy trying to prove myself. After a few minutes, I forgot all about it. We wrapped up the job, loaded up our gear, and headed back to quarters.

We got back to the firehouse and, as we finished cleaning up our gear and getting ready for chow, I felt a little bit of a throbbing pain settling into my leg. I didn't think much of it at the time. I'd spent some time on the treadmill earlier in the day and did a little heavier lifting in the weight room than I normally did. I was thinking maybe I pulled a hamstring.

Sidenote- If you ever find yourself looking to tour firehouses in Chicago and you're near Albany Park, head over to Engine 124's house on the corner of Montrose and Kedzie. Ask to see the hole in the wall and make sure you buy a T-shirt. Don't go between 1 and 3 though, that's when the guys are studying for the promotional exams.

We wrapped up dinner and started turning in for the night. It actually ended up being a quiet night and we got to sleep through, which was rare. Engine 124's house is home to the Engine, Truck 38 (my first and favorite assignment), the Chief for the 10th Battalion, Ambulance 32 and the jump wagon (a rig with a giant inflatable bag meant to save someone jumping off of a building). So there were more than a few rigs that could be called out at any time. The next morning as I rolled out of my bunk, any idea that I had a pulled hammy was out the window. I could barely put any weight on my right leg. It took everything I had to get myself out to the car after I was relieved from duty.

When I was 24 years old, I was diagnosed with severe herniation of the L5-S1 and L4-L5 with a bulging disc at L3-L4. I spent the better part of the next two months off work, going to physical therapy and walking with a cane. Thankfully, the benefits I had covered my time off and I was able to focus on recovery. The first orthopedic surgeon took one look at my MRI and told me very matter-of-factly that I needed to have a double fusion. I refused to accept this. I was too young for this to happen. There had to be other options. It took me another five or six years of meeting with neurosurgeons, chiropractors, massage therapists, and any other specialty I could think of to find the solution that ultimately worked for me. In the meantime, I stumbled across a pain management specialist. It started with epidural cortisone injections. The first one gave me some relief for about six months. That was coupled with high doses of naproxen. Within a couple of years, I was taking 8 Aleve a day and going in for injections every 4 to 6 weeks.

There was a concern that high dosages of the medications I was taking could start causing serious liver damage, so I was prescribed Norco, a combination of oxycodone and acetaminophen. Over the course of the next two years, I slowly began to spiral out of control. Opioid addiction is insidious. You don't realize you're addicted. You're not trying to get high. You're following doctor's orders. You build a tolerance and your mind tricks you into thinking you need more. One pill a day turned into two. Two pills turned into four. Four pills turned into eight. It didn't take long before it started taking a toll.

Shae: I was eighteen years old when I moved from my parents' house in Ohio to Chicago to be with Ryan. This is probably not what most parents want their daughter to do, being that I met Ryan on spring break just five months prior and now I was moving out of state to live with him. In my defense, I had conditions if I was going to move and live with Ryan. One was that I absolutely had to get a college education. I was to take a year off schooling after high school (which I highly recommend by the way!) and then go to college.

I came from a middle-class family. My dad is entrepreneurial and my mom is a very hard worker. They always told of the importance of owning a home and a business. They never pressured me to go to college, nor offered to pay for it, but it was something that I was set on doing. Ryan supported this plan. I mostly worked part time while attending college and that was because I could lean on Ryan. He invested in me even back then. It helped that I was very passionate about what I was pursuing which was interior design. I love creating spaces. As a child, I provided interior design services to my Barbies. In my teens, I talked my friends into helping me repaint my room twice.

Four years after we got married, I got my Bachelor's Degree in Interior Design. At this time, we both just had our heads down grinding away. In 2012 we bought our first home. It was a Chicago bungalow on the northwest side. It was the dead of winter in February and an estate sale home that didn't show well. It was a diamond in the rough and Ryan and I knew it instantly. Looking back, we also think it may have been haunted, but that's a story for over a campfire! The home was built in 1916 and it was pretty large. It had five bedrooms, two bathrooms, and a full unfinished basement. There were copious amounts of wall paper, lime green plaid looking vinyl floors in the kitchen, and some original electrical wrapped in cloth. When we went to redo the sunroom, we tore out the floor and found newspapers from 1929 that were used as insulation! We transformed that place with a small budget. In the three years we lived there we scraped wall paper, refinished floors, painted cabinets, and replaced hardware and fixtures. We landscaped the front and back, replaced the roof (insurance claim), and polished it up to a home we could be proud of. We figure we spent about $20k.

The year we purchased our first home is also when I graduated college and birthed our first child. Everything that happened in 2012 set the motion for our major struggles in 2013 that rocked our marriage, our world, and changed our mindsets forever. We were in our mid-late twenties but up until this point we were really still just kids.

The exact day we started moving into our home in 2012, I started having a miscarriage. We were devastated. We found out I was pregnant (this was my last semester of college) and instantly fell in love with our "little tadpole." I will never forget how cold the doctor was when she confirmed what was happening and that we were losing our baby. I will never forget how I felt in the days after when I would see a mom pushing her young child in the cart at the grocery store. Everywhere I looked I was reminded of what we had lost. I was taking finals while attending two different colleges, I took as many classes as I could at the less expensive community college, and we were in the middle of moving into our first home. I cried and grieved some but taking time off wasn't an option. Then just one month later I found out I was pregnant again with our son Gavin, who is now ten years old. I wish I could say I was *fixed* after successfully carrying my son to term so soon after the miscarriage, but I was actually just...frozen. I had fallen into depression. I was too scared to be happy about being pregnant and began feeling withdrawn. I spent my pregnancy putting walls up around myself. I struggled with my identity after finally getting that college degree that I wanted so badly while also being a new mom. This would later manifest itself into a bit of substance abuse, reckless behavior and a certain level of detachment from the ones I loved.

Ryan was battling his own demons at the same time. Thinking back, my husband was a much different person then. His fire for life, passions, and creativity were being watered down. He was in pain, addicted to narcotics, and facing major surgeries that would make it so he'd need to sit behind a desk instead of being a first responder. We were investing very little into our relationship at this time. We were both in pain and didn't know how to cope nor how to help one another.

Meanwhile, our credit card debt was catching up to us, remember how I said we liked to travel and go out, and we were really struggling financially. We were fighting a lot, nearly separated, and totally disconnected. We were in a deep hole with our marriage, spiritually, financially, physically, and mentally. This hole took about three years to dig and we were about as low as it could go. Ultimately, we knew we wanted to spend the rest of our lives together but we desperately needed to reconnect. We decided to get help. *Time to get up and figure this all out!*

We started seeing a therapist - both individually and for our marriage. Shae got help for her depression. We came up with a game plan for Ryan's back surgery. We started reading self-help books. We sold our house and made an amazing profit! We were able to pay off our seventy thousand dollars in credit card debt and rent an apartment with twenty-five thousand dollars left. We decided we wanted to move out of Chicago, which is why we rented instead of bought at that time. A visit to Colorado followed by a visit to the Ozarks made our souls happy and we needed mountains. We made visits to both areas, scheming our move.

Ryan still needed back surgery however and the fire dept had great insurance. He was waiting on a specific prosthetic disc to clear the FDA (it was already being used in Germany and Sweden). The alternative was to fuse 2 levels of his spine together and, as a young man, he was rightfully concerned this would affect his mobility for the rest of his life. Meanwhile he was stuck in immense pain: picture a twenty-something walking with a cane, getting monthly steroid injections and taking strong narcotics just to get by.

We were prepared to take a trip out of the country so he could get the prosthetics. Right before we booked our tickets, his neurosurgeon called him with some good news. The state-of-the-art discs had been approved for use in the US! The catch was that they could only do one at a time and Ryan needed two. This meant two surgeries, one year apart. It was still good news though. Ryan got his first disc replacement surgery shortly after. The relief was immediate! He was walking, standing straighter, and in less pain than he'd been in years - just days after surgery! He was then able to get some help and get off the painkillers.

He was physically ill for a couple of weeks, it was a difficult road, but that fire of determination was starting to rekindle! This was the first time in years Shae had seen a glimmer of the man she fell in love with. It was like a fog was lifting. The storm clouds were parting and we were on the cusp of taking charge of our own lives again, together.

Ryan was able to take a year of paid leave at the Chicago Fire Department for surgery and recovery. Meanwhile, we had decided that the Ozarks is where we wanted to be. We bought a second home (even though we did not own a primary!) in 2016 near Table Rock Lake and were able to use Ryan's fire department income to secure the mortgage. We ultimately knew we were going to relocate even though the rural fire departments do not pay like Chicago (also we didn't know if it would work with Ryan's back) and, with a population of under fifteen thousand residents, we assumed Branson would not be the best place for Shae's interior design talents (which we now know wasn't accurate). We didn't care about this uncertainty. We knew that we were both smart and that we would figure it out.

We were on the same team again and we wanted to build something together. We were ready for the fresh start and the fresh air! People thought we were crazy for moving from Chicago to Omaha, Arkansas. When we made this decision, Ryan had great income and an excellent pension plan with the CFD and Shae's interior design career was taking off. We had to do this though and we were both all in - three-year-old Gavin too! Little Gavin loved that he could pee on trees in his new country life.

A fresh start and change of scenery had us feeling recharged. There was still something missing from our lives though. We were both raised to consider ourselves Christians, but, throughout the course of our relationship, we had not once gone to church together. We had never prayed together. We really did not invite God into our lives at all.

After our big move, Ryan still had one more back surgery lined up (the third and final), we had to reinvent ourselves socially and professionally five hundred and fifty miles away from where we had called home, and we were struggling with infertility.

We had been trying for our second child for almost two years with no success. In the year leading up to the move, we met regularly with a fertility specialist, tried a number of medical interventions, and followed doctor's orders. It was starting to seem futile.

A few months after getting settled into the new house we saw a Facebook post for an open house at First Baptist Church in Branson. They were going to have a bounce house, games, and activities for kids in the community. This seemed like a good opportunity to get out of the house and let Gavin meet some new friends.

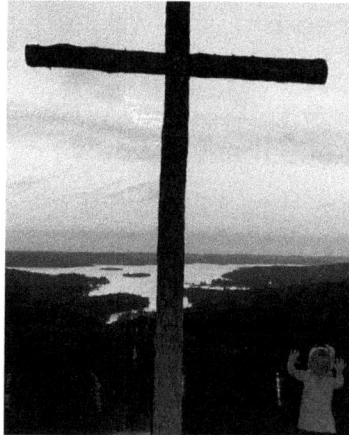

Prayer

Towards the end of the event, we found ourselves directed down the hall towards the exits where members of the church were waiting to introduce themselves and offer to sit with us in prayer. This was completely out of our comfort zone. We weren't church people. We didn't pray. There was something different in this moment though. When Chris looked at us and asked if there was anything that we wanted to pray for, we didn't hesitate. We wanted another child. For the first time as a couple, we came together in prayer and asked the Lord to bless us with our second baby. That Sunday was the first time we attended a church service together. The following week, we had a positive pregnancy test. Lana Mae Duffy was born in August of 2017.

Moving to the Ozarks was one of the best decisions we have ever made. I absolutely believe God led us here. We were able to heal spiritually, emotionally, and physically in ways that, just a few years earlier, we would've thought impossible.

We've since come to realize just how important a foundation of faith is to having a successful marriage and a business. When presented with difficult decisions or uncomfortable situations, being able to lean into that pillar of belief is absolutely critical.

Growth

Ryan: In 2017 I was recovering from my last surgery which was my second disc replacement. At this time, Shae was working on building her business as a real estate agent while being pregnant with Lana.

After having two total disc replacements, I started working in construction. Shae's uncle had been a general contractor for years and was looking for someone to help him build a house for a client on land that he was developing. Seems a little counterintuitive but honestly, after years of pain and limited mobility, swinging a hammer every day felt amazing. I couldn't lift anything over fifty or sixty pounds, and I had to be very mindful of how I moved, but it still felt good and provided a steady income while Shae was getting her business off the ground.

Over the course of the next year, I learned how to build a house literally from the ground up. We laid out the footers and built our own forms for the crawlspace walls. We did all of the concrete work. We framed it up and ran all of the plumbing and electrical. We put on the steel roof and insulated the home. The client wanted concrete log siding that was cast from forms created out of the actual logs used to build an 1800s log cabin in Tennessee. We had those shipped in and sided the house to look like it was an actual log home, without the inefficiencies and maintenance requirements that come with having a log home. The only things we didn't do was install the septic system, drill the well, the HVAC, and drywall. Those specialties we subcontracted out. I didn't make much money that year but the education was invaluable. I just had a crash course in what it takes to be a general contractor.

In 2018, I became a licensed home builder specializing in residential remodels. I partnered up with my neighbor Randy, who had also recently relocated to the area from Illinois. I knew there was a demand for contractors in our area but I had no idea how much of a need there was for it until we put ourselves out there looking for jobs. I remember someone telling me as I was just getting started, that if I answer my phone and keep my word that I would be as busy as I want to be. That proved to be true. It seemed that a lot of workers in the area had a tendency to turn their phones off when it was hunting season or the fish were biting, and there is a lot of good hunting and fishing in the Ozarks.

I was focused on building my business and learning new skills. I never turned down the opportunity to bid on a job, even if it was further away than I wanted to drive or it involved something that I wasn't familiar with. There were a few times I would walk through the home with the client and, as I was calmly taking notes and photos, I would be racking my brain trying to figure out if I had the capacity to do the job I was looking at. I'd go back home and spend the next few nights watching YouTube videos on how to do the part of the project I didn't have experience in. If I still felt uncomfortable or unable to properly bid the job, I would try to sub it out.

We found ourselves booked up six months out at any given time and were struggling to keep up with the workload. Our reputation was starting to become established in the community and I didn't have enough time to accommodate all of the jobs coming our way. I started trying to talk Shae into giving up on real estate to help me out with the construction business. She had done quite a bit of estimating and design work while we lived in Chicago. She had been a licensed agent for two years and it seemed to me we would make more money if she came to help me in my business. She was barely making anything in real estate despite working nearly full time with a baby on her hip.

She stuck to her guns insisting that her hard work was going to start paying off. She had been "planting seeds" and nurturing her business diligently for the past twenty-four months. Her reputation was starting to take hold in the community as well. People realized that Shae was hard working, cared about her clients, and had a skillset that most other agents do not possess. She was an experienced interior designer with first-hand experience in remodels and construction.

Within six months of trying to convince her to quit, we had turned our primary residence into a short-term rental (STR) called The Crystal Cabin. Randy and his wife Tammy partnered with us to buy a shop house down the road where we would move our family into so we could flip our primary to a rental. That little house was a gold mine. Within the first few weeks of going up on Airbnb, the revenue stream being created by that three-bedroom home was surpassing what I was bringing home each month working ten to twelve hours a day in construction. I knew that I needed to focus on STRs. I got my real estate license in 2019 and shortly after Shae was pregnant with baby number three.

Shae: After moving from Chicago to Omaha, AR just outside of Branson, I searched for design gigs constantly. I would look on Craigslist, network with contractors, and ultimately got my real estate license because I figured there would be a decent chance one of these homeowners would need design services. In Chicago, my design business had started taking off and I had no problem finding work. People were starting to come to me. In Branson, it didn't take long for me to realize that I was the new kid in town and I had zero clients. I was also inexperienced as a realtor and had no sales stats to point to. That was a blow to my ego, I must admit, but I was determined. I had a great mentor, Tammy Rodman, that helped me with lead generating and prospecting. I began calling *For Sale by Owners* and door knocking. At one point, I was 8 months pregnant in July and was knocking on doors. Those methods may be old school, and not very fun, but they do work! I went above and beyond and used my design background to stage my listings at no extra charge.

One time I spent half a day in a furnished vacant home moving and rearranging things. My clients became raving fans and would recommend me to their friends and also enthusiastically recommend me all over social media. Finally, I was getting calls from people just because they would see how highly recommended I was from others. I barely made anything the first two years but in my third year my sales quadrupled and part of that was when I switched brokerages and received mentorship from Jeramie Worley. Ultimately, I recruited Ryan onto my team and then Kenya Wilhite, and now we have our own brokerage with nine agents including me and Ryan.

Now

As of today, we own our own real estate brokerage specializing in short-term rental, lake, and development called Duffy Homes Realty. We are also licensed home builders, catering to a niche custom market in North Arkansas called Duffy Homes LLC. We also personally own, operate, and manage for others short-term rental properties through our property management business: Ozark Mountain Vacation.

Why?

We fell in love with the Ozarks. There is a certain quality to this part of the world that is hard to put into words. Starry skies. Fresh air. Friendly people. Nature. Lake. Freedom. Faith.

Everyone who owns a vacation rental seems to want a piece of what we have here. Over the past few years, developers have done very well by taking unrestricted lakeview land and cramming in as many homes as they can with zero lot line separations (standalone condos).

We've known for years that the beautiful peninsula we live on is prime for development and that someone would start building on it soon. We realized that if we want to build a community we would be proud to have our children grow into, we need to ensure it is developed in such a way that maintains the characteristics that we cherish for generations to come.

Our mission is to responsibly guide the development of our community. We strive to create developments that preserve the natural beauty of the land while preventing oversaturation, from both a business and community perspective. In so doing, we can create amenities and improvements that can be enjoyed by the entire community, not just vacation rental investors. Privately funded community parks, school bus stops, and neighborhood trash cleanups are the beginning of that vision.

NETWORKING

It is really important to talk to people. This may be out of your comfort zone, but it is crucial. Find your style. Become a member of a club or a school board, play golf, chat with a stranger, befriend other parents at your child's school. This doesn't mean you don't be genuine and certainly don't go into a relationship thinking *What's in it for me?* but instead think of *What can I contribute to others and how can we help each other?*

Relationships are everything.

Between Shae being a real estate agent and Ryan being a contractor, we were always networking and looking to make connections. One day on her way home, Shae noticed a new neighbor moving into the area. She stopped her car and got out and introduced herself and welcomed them. They exchanged business cards and now we have someone to refer to for foundation repair. That same neighbor gave Shae a heads up that the owner of the house next to our shop house or "shouse" wanted to sell. This is all right down the road from our cash cow, the Crystal Cabin. Shae called the owner right away and got a meeting. We bought the house with our partners Randy and Tammy and did flip-into-STR part two.

This one we paid one hundred and fifty-five thousand dollars and put about sixty thousand dollars into material and furnishings for a major remodel. We did the labor ourselves over the course of about six months. This was during COVID, so it was a little scary. We knew if tourism took a dive that it would also make a good long-term rental, so it was a smart buy that definitely needed remodeling. Most of the furniture we procured from estate sales and Facebook marketplace.

Here is a tip: befriend people that own estate sale businesses!

This house became the Ruby Retreat (see the gem stone theme!) and it grossed over seventy thousand dollars in a nine-month period. *BOOM! WE DID IT AGAIN!*

Our friends and partners ended up jumping on an opportunity to buy some beautiful acreage about an hour away and we decided to sell the Ruby Retreat. Simultaneously, we had the opportunity to buy twenty-seven acres at the end of our peninsula where we could build our dream home and get out of the Shouse. We decided to sell the Crystal Cabin that same year.

For the Ruby Retreat, since it was an investment property, we had to take our proceeds and buy another investment property in order to avoid paying capital gains tax. The proceeds from the Crystal Cabin were a different story. We had lived in it for two consecutive years within the last five years so we didn't pay a dime in taxes on that gain, which was substantial. The profit from both these flips were crazy. *Why was it so substantial?* We turned so-so single-family homes in an emerging market into a beautifully decorated cash machine. Investors will pay top dollar for a turn key property. We see these types of substantial gains all the time when we have our realtor hats on too. The property that is under-performing, not performing, or in an emerging market are the ones to look for.

We have a real estate brokerage with 9 agents, a construction and development business that specializes in unique STR builds, and a property management company. We are finishing up construction on a container home that we anticipate will be the highest performing three-bedroom STR in the Branson market. Mike and Julie, our friends and colleagues, had five acres with killer views of Table Rock Lake with no restrictions. They essentially handed Ryan the keys as a real estate broker and budding developer to sell their property. Ryan had them clear it to show the views, then market the individual lots as custom STR build lots where he would broker the deal and then build the product.

Once the container home started taking shape, the development sold out and our friends did very well. This container home build project has been one of the riskiest yet biggest boosts to our business. It is not less expensive than a conventional build and they are difficult to finance, especially if there's none in the area to compare it to which was our case. We ended up taking equity out of the Emerald Escape, which is property we'd bought with a 1031 Exchange when we'd sold the Ruby Retreat. We knew that we didn't have enough money to comfortably finish the build, but we did it anyway. We had faith that we could sell it because it was unique and cool and no one else has an STR like it in our area.

At networking events, we have people coming up to us talking about how cool it is and there is even some national exposure. We ended up getting two investors to get an equity stake in it so we were able to get some pressure off while we finished it out. While Shae put her design touches on it, the container home was Ryan's baby. Shae had to really put a lot of faith in Ryan (and the Lord!) and Ryan thanks her almost daily for trusting in his wild idea. While we would be lying if we said we've not had some heated discussions about the pressure it has put on us financially, it has become a testament to our support for each other and how powerful we are when we work together as a team.

Build Project

We have a pretty full slate for future projects. In addition to our personal home build and the container home that are happening simultaneously, we are also breaking ground on a resort that we hold a one third equity stake in called The Constellations. It will be adult only luxury A Frames with a community indoor pool that we will have exclusive management rights to. There's nothing else like it in our market.

The other projects involve developing in such a way that gives back to our community. Everything we are doing is in one area of Omaha, Arkansas where it borders Table Rock Lake. We live here and will continue to live here. While development in this area is inevitable due to its proximity to Branson, we want to have a significant influence over the direction it goes so that we do not destroy what makes it special. The area is rural with a mix of nice country homes and some run-down homes.

We focus on lifting up the areas that are run down or, if we do build on vacant land, we ensure the types of builds fit into what is already around it. We have made a point to get to know our neighbors and we regularly mail letters to landowners asking if they want to sell.

One of the projects coming up will offer new construction builds for VA (veteran) home buyers and they will be ADA accessible homes. We also will be creating a community park that will be maintained via a not-for-profit camping area. There are some other new construction STR projects in the works as well that all have private one acre lots with a creek, which is unlike most options in the Branson market. Our management arm, Ozark Mountain Vacations, will manage all of these and it's all within five minutes of our house. The location of our management operations and office will be where we are currently living, the Shouse. It is amazing how it all comes full circle in just four years.

One of our continued challenges is the work life balance. We have flexible schedules but feel like we are always working. We have embraced it somewhat and we incorporate our children into our business and we explain to them what we are doing. We let them hear our conversations, our strategies, our fears, and our praise to one another as partners and as spouses. We ask them to help us with some management duties and sometimes we even hire them to help (well not the two year old yet!). We just left a hotel this morning and our ten-year-old hand wrote them a review! It was actually a proud moment to see how observant he is and how he felt compelled to compliment the remodel but let them know about an issue in a way that was respectful.

My five-year-old daughter has over $100 saved up and she says she is going to save it up to buy a business or a "golden office." Our efforts enable us to send them to a private school and for us to be involved with their school. We were able to gift Shae's parent's a half-acre with a run-down garage and then help them get it turned into an income producing cabin which will contribute significantly to their retirement, which was a source of anxiety for them as they age. We can't help but notice the more we give back, the more the Lord provides.

We could not have planned the series of events that has led us down this path to creating generational wealth in such a short time. The question about "what is your five-year plan" has always been difficult to answer because we tend to jump at the opportunities as they present themselves and then those opportunities lead us down paths that we didn't know existed. We lean on our faith when a door opens and we believe in ourselves and in each other's abilities to create the best plan. It is scary, it is exciting, it is rewarding, and it is even a little addicting!

AVOIDING ANALYSIS PARALYSIS

This is **KEY**. Every change in your life and your career requires learning a new skill, leaving your comfort zone, and leaning into your faith and relationships.

- Do not let yourself fall into the trap of complacency.
- Do not tell yourself something is too hard.
- Do not sabotage your success by telling yourself you don't have the skills needed to achieve your goals.
- You can learn.

Look for a need in your market. It doesn't matter what industry you're in. There is always an opportunity to build a better mousetrap. I've always been inspired by Mike Rowe (host of the hit show Dirty Jobs). Mike had a message a few years ago where he said "Don't follow your passion." His speech was fascinating. "Just because you're passionate about something doesn't mean you won't suck at it." He tells an anecdote about a very successful business owner who stated to him that "I looked around to see where everyone else was headed, and then I went the opposite way." He goes on to say "Follow opportunity, not passion and the passion will follow."

When we moved to the Ozarks, we had to reinvent ourselves. Ryan was a firefighter in the city of Chicago for 9 years and Shae had owned an interior design business. We knew that we couldn't earn the same level of income with these jobs in this area as we were accustomed to in a large urban economy, so we looked for a new path.

When we sold our first home in Chicago, we realized that real estate investing was a path to success. We saw a six-figure return on our three-year investment and learned after the fact that since it had been our primary residence for at least two years, we were exempt from capital gains tax. This single event provided the catalyst for our next big step in life. We were able to pay off all of our debt and have a nest egg for the first time in our lives.

Then we purchased our second home and our first in the Ozarks. The process was awful. We had a mortgage broker who dropped the ball repeatedly along with a real estate agent who made several errors and omissions throughout the process of our purchase costing us a good deal of stress and added expense above and beyond our five hundred and fifty mile move with a toddler. We saw our next opportunity. Shae said she could be a better realtor.

Real estate school, as we came to find out, was a lot like other schools that we had gone through for the purpose of state licensure. It didn't teach you how to be a great realtor. You have to figure that out on your own. Shae spent the next year or so with a large nationally recognized real estate brokerage trying to learn how to be the best agent she could be and best serve her clients to grow her business.

We live, work, and develop very close to Branson, Missouri. Branson is an established vacation rental investment market, with ever changing regulations, restrictions, and tax implications for these types of investments. People were wanting to invest in short-term rentals and Shae didn't know how to serve them.

Her broker at the time couldn't offer the education she needed, so she looked for the area expert. This is how we met Jeramie and Kelly Worley.

Shae transferred her license to Worley and Associates and within a matter of months, EVERYTHING changed. We had the mentorship we needed to have the confidence to move out of our home and convert it into our first income producing property.

When Ryan started his construction business, there was a HUGE learning curve. This was a new career for him. He had spent the previous nine years destroying homes working on a fire department truck company and now he was learning to build homes. He was blessed to have the opportunity to work with Shae's uncle, who was an experienced general contractor, and build two homes from the ground up. He was literally hands-on for every aspect of the build from foundation to finish.

When he went on to residential remodel work, Ryan would go to do an estimate and then spend the next few nights scouring YouTube watching videos about how other contractors would go about the job before committing to a bid or feeling confident in his ability to accept it.

When we started our brokerage, we had to lean into our agents. Ryan had to spend hours going through the necessary licensing courses for the various states we were operating in. At the same time, we had to keep the lights on.

This is where Marty and Kenya come into the mix. Kenya was an agent with us when we had our team at Worley & Associates. Her husband Marty joined us just before we moved on to start our own brokerage. They have been our saving grace. Through times of uncertainty and change, we knew we could count on them to serve our clients with a level of professionalism and expertise that we could be proud of. Without their help, we wouldn't have had the margin in our schedules to grow our various businesses.

AS A COUPLE

Don't let animosity take hold. It's a total cliche, but it's true. Don't go to sleep angry. You need to make sure you're both communicating. Minor annoyances can grow into major issues within your relationship if you let them grow.

Make time for your relationship. These points sound pretty basic but they can be easy to overlook when you've got your head down trying to work through the trenches.

When you combine your business and home life, things can get complicated. Make sure you keep an open dialogue with your partner. If you have concerns or apprehensions about something that the other person is doing, or not doing, communicate it. However, don't hold each other back. Shae could have easily said no when Ryan wanted to build the container home. In fact, it would have been perfectly logical for her to do so. However, she had faith in Ryan and knew that if they could pull it off that it would lead to bigger opportunities.

Plan date nights. If you can't work it into the schedule, make time for short day dates. Go out to lunch or just make a point of being together while you collectively work on something. Quality time with your partner doesn't have to be spent around a candle lit table. They can just as easily be three hours together in the hardware store as you fill up four carts trying to wrap up your latest project. Just make sure you do it together.

SHORT TERM RENTALS

For the past few years, STRs have been about the hottest thing in real estate for many investors. If you had short-term rental properties in 2021 and 2022, odds are you were seeing amazing returns. In that same period of time, there has been a parade of social media influencer's, real estate agents and property managers encouraging investors to jump into the game.

Q&A: Can you create substantial wealth through short-term rental investments? *Absolutely!* Is it passive income? *Absolutely not.*

Don't let anyone convince you otherwise. The STR gold rush following Covid is over. If you want to be profitable in your business, you have to put in the work. Increased competition in the marketplace, rising interest rates and a stabilizing of the artificially inflated demand that we saw in the past couple of years is making it so that the margins are narrower.

When you are looking at your next, or first, STR investment, make sure you are running the numbers thoroughly. Make sure you are doing it SEVERAL times, taking into account a number of different variables and assumptions of your potential rate of return. Don't just look at the pro forma the property manager gave you, or the rental history provided by a realtor. Just because the person with all of the TikTok followers says it's a great deal doesn't mean it is.

Find an area that has positive growth trends and identify a property that has a high level of potential for improvement. New construction or remodel projects (think BRRRR) have a much higher potential return on investment than turn-key properties. They require more work, but once you put in the effort you can create systems to manage your property and create a significant flow of income while growing the equity of your asset.

If you're not familiar with the Buy, Remodel, Rent, Reappraise and Repeat (BRRRR) Method, start looking into it. That is how we were able to finance our last three investment projects on the value of one single property.

BUY: When we sold our second investment property, the Ruby Retreat, we used the profit we made to reinvest using a 1031 tax deferred exchange to purchase what is now the Emerald Escape. The down payment amount was substantial and we had quite a bit of equity in the home from day one. We pulled a home equity line of credit (HELOC) on the house to finance the improvements we knew that it needed to become a successful short-term rental.

REMODEL: We spent the next six months completely renovating the home. We replaced a load way with a beam to create an open concept. We relocated the entry door, added windows to showcase the lakeview, added a fourth bedroom, added a bathroom, and moved the staircase. It was a big project that added substantial value to the home.

RENT: Once the home was remodeled and furnished, we put it up as a short-term rental. The Emerald Escape became a cash flowing asset. Then it was time to assess the value.

REAPPRAISE: We paid to have a new appraisal done on the home. The result was fantastic. The home was worth more than two hundred thousand dollars above what we paid for it just six months before. Our HELOC amount just jumped up significantly. It was time to do it again.

REPEAT: We used the HELOC to tear the detached garage that was on the property down to the foundation and rebuild it as a standalone couple's cabin. We tied it into the city water line, put in a septic system, and set it up as a STR. Our total investment in that project was about ninety thousand dollars. It appraised for two hundred and nine thousand dollars and is cash flowing incredibly well. Time to repeat again and start building a shipping container home!

The purchase of one property (the Emerald Escape) over the course of the next eighteen months, led to owning two more investment properties by strategically utilizing the equity we already had built in.

CREATING A LIFE OF ABUNDANCE AS A FAMILY

Family Photo

We work incredibly hard to reach our ever-changing goals. This requires long hours and sacrifice but we try to incorporate our family into our business as much as possible. While it's not always practical to bring your kids to work, if you do it regularly the education they receive is incredible.

We've brought our kids to client meetings. We make a point of bringing them to the job sites at our construction projects and make sure they pay attention to the conversations we're having with our contractors. We openly discuss our finances in front of them and explain how we are investing and reinvesting what we earn. They don't always like it but the lessons we are instilling in our children are more valuable than anything they will learn in school.

We've never given our kids an allowance but if they want something badly enough, we give them the opportunity to earn it. Gavin mows our lawns and has a road side shop that he's built to sell rocks and gems that he finds on our property. Lana, seeing the success that Gavin has selling his rocks, sells lemonade next to him (Lana's Lemons). Our two-year-old Jack just takes it all in. Our children may not choose to follow the same paths as we did but we want to ensure that they learn the skills they need to be entrepreneurs if they choose to be. Most importantly, they will see us working together as a couple and we will be able to share these lessons together as a family.

Here is a testimonial we just received from Mike and Julie M.:

"The first time I met Shae Duffy, she was an enthusiastic, positive, and very pregnant professional. She had a passion for her business, that even then, included her family. Shortly after, we met her husband Ryan, with their oldest son. Ryan talked to us about opportunities, for improvement, in our community, while holding his son's hand. They love their community, and have a desire to improve, and expand, to make it, not only a better place for their neighbors, but a wonderful area for their children to thrive, and grow. Their commitment to their business, would only slightly pale, to their unwavering support, and love, for their children, and each other. They truly are an example, that you can have it all, if you put family and each other first. "

Scan the QR code below to watch our interview on Youtube!

ACKNOWLEDGMENTS

From Shae & Ryan Duffy

We would like to give thanks to our parents first and foremost. You were the original power couples that helped pave the way for where we are today. Looking back, we see the sacrifices you made for your children, your families and each other. Each set of parents had very different styles and dynamics yet both households were full of love and togetherness. It wasn't always sunshine and rainbows, but you were able to persevere and ride it out through thick and thin. Both sets of parents have been married since before we were born and are now the most amazing grandparents. How lucky we are!

The mentorship, encouragement and faith in us from our friends and colleagues has been instrumental in opening new doors. You truly are who you surround yourself with and we have been blessed to be acquainted with so many wonderful entrepreneurial couples. Randy and Tammy Martin supported and invested in our crazy idea to turn our primary residence into an STR. Jeramie and Kelly Worley provided mentorship and education into the world of investing in vacation rentals. Mike and Julie Mecke believed in our vision and gave us carte blanche for their land sales and development which has propelled us to participate in the endeavors we're working on today. Thank you for investing in us!

To Marty and Kenya Wilhite: Thank you!!! We could not be where we are in our careers if it weren't for you. We are SO blessed to have you in our lives. The trust, collaboration and friendship we have with you mean the world to us.

To our children Gavin, Lana and Jack: we dedicate our lives and our legacies to you. It is our sincerest hope that we are able to instill a lasting foundation of service, faith and the spirit of entrepreneurialism to you three.

Meghan and Andrew, thank you for putting this project together and for giving us the opportunity to be a part of it. We truly appreciate the chance to share our story. We hope that it may help inspire others. Neither one of us came from wealthy families and we have leaned on each other to create a level of business partnership in our marriage. This partnership is on track to create generational wealth through real estate investing.

ABOUT THE AUTHORS:
Shae & Ryan Duffy

Shae and Ryan met by chance in the spring of 2005 on the white sands of Panama City Beach, Florida. At the time, Shae was a senior in high school living in Xenia, Ohio and Ryan was stationed at Fort Polk, Louisiana. This encounter led to a long-distance relationship leading to Shae moving to Chicago to be with Ryan once he came home from Louisiana. They returned to Panama City Beach on June 26, 2008 to be married on the beach surrounded by their families. Ryan went on to join the Chicago Fire Department while Shae pursued an education and career in interior design. The years following the initial "honeymoon" period were filled with trials. Experiencing debilitating injury, addiction, loss, and depression as a young couple stressed their marriage near the breaking point. A bold move and new found faith brought them back together as a stronger couple, setting the foundation for an inspiring business relationship.

Ryan Duffy is a real estate broker, home builder, and property manager specializing in STR properties near Branson, Missouri. Following a series of back injuries sustained during his career as a Chicago Firefighter, Ryan (along with his incredibly talented and beautiful wife Shae) decided to give up city life in pursuit of star filled skies, lake life, and a quieter country setting to raise their family. Their firm, Duffy Homes Realty, assists clients in the sale and acquisition of investment properties as well as offering guidance on the development

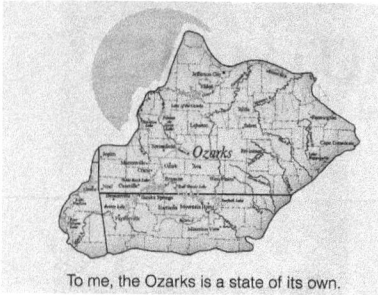

To me, the Ozarks is a state of its own.

of their land. In the fall of 2019, Ryan and Shae founded Ozark Mountain Vacations, which has grown into a collection of short-term rental properties and five-star management in Omaha, Arkansas near Table Rock Lake. While most Branson area accommodations are crowded into large condo or resort settings, Ozark Mountain Vacations breaks the mold by offering individual single-family homes on larger lots with private amenities. This enables guests to reconnect with nature and each other while still being just a short drive from major area attractions. Through their construction business Duffy Homes LLC, Ryan and Shae are creating purpose-built developments focused on preserving the look, feel, and values that drew them to the Ozarks. The Duffys pride themselves on supporting others in their investment journey and emphasize the transformational nature of smart real estate investment for individual families and communities as a whole.

HTTPS://LINKTR.EE/DUFFYHOMES

SWIPING RIGHT CHANGED OUR LIVES

BY DAVE AND KIM MENAPACE

If you look at our lives today, you'll see a couple in their mid-30s with two young kids, a dog, a house in the burbs, two vacation homes, and a young, but thriving business. You'd think we have it all figured out, but we'll be honest here; we have daily struggles managing it all. We often refer to that struggle as acting like *a duck above water* as we try our darndest to make everything on the surface seem calm, cool and collected, but under the surface are paddling furiously to build that life we've dreamed of.

Ten years ago, at the age of 25, we met on a dating app while living in Boston. And it wasn't just any dating app, but Tinder specifically. Now before you judge, we know that this dating app has a reputation for being for, ahem, casual dating and not serious long-term relationships. However, that wasn't the case for us. We had known several friends who met their now spouses on the app, and noticed that they had a mutual friend in common; someone Dave had gone to high school with had had also gone to school with Kim at Boston College. We decided to give it a go and went on our first date on a Wednesday night in late August of 2013. Dave brought a Bertucci's pizza and wine and Kim brought cookies from Flour bakery and we met on the dock at the esplanade of Boston's Back Bay neighborhood overlooking the Charles River. There were several groups of friends and couples on the dock that night and as we talked and listened to country music for hours and it began to lightly rain, we didn't even realize that we were the last ones there, slow dancing to our favorite country songs deep into the night. We have been together ever since that night.

Our relationship took lots of twists and turns over the next couple years including a cross-country move to Los Angeles for Dave's job, getting two Great Dane puppies, both of us completing our Master's Degrees, and a few job changes for each of us. Eventually we got married and bought a home in Dave's hometown of Holliston, MA. Our care and responsibility-free lives of our mid-20s had transformed into a more mature state of being by the time we broached 30 and we were expecting our first child in the summer of 2019. Throughout this time, especially during the home buying process for our primary home, we frequently talked about what we did and didn't want for the trajectory of our lives and for our children. We knew we didn't want to live beyond our means. We also knew we wanted to have a greater than average life.

When you combine these two, that meant that we wanted to reach a level of financial success that exceeds the middle class, but to keep our expenses in check enough that it was never triggering and causing stress. Lifestyle creep is very real. There are unavoidable expenses you must incur, like childcare costs if you both plan to still work, and then there are optional decisions like upgrading your house or car. Our plan to combat lifestyle creep was to widen the delta between what we make and what we spend so much that we would never worry. Furthermore, we wanted to live a life of generosity, giving to those around us and to charities alike.

Dave and Kim vacationing at Mammoth Mountain for the holidays while newly engaged and living in Los Angeles, CA. This is now their photo on their Airbnb host profile.

Longer term, we also wanted to own vacation properties to enjoy in the present and pass down to the family in the future. Kim's family rented a beach house in Duxbury, MA and that home felt like their own, even though they were just renters. Dave recalled trips to the Finger Lakes in New York while growing up where his grandparents rented a cabin for the summer. We dreamed of owning homes like these so we'd never have to give them up. Those memories would return with each new visit to the home and then we'd add to those memories with new ones. We'd never have to worry about the owners selling or deciding to stop renting because it was ours now. That was the sentimental and *let's take control of our own destiny* side of our motivation. The other side of it was us being a little salty hearing countless accounts of people now middle-aged saying that they would have, could have, should have bought that vacation home or that rental property and we were determined for that not to be us. When you compound the vacation experiences, the cash flow and the equity growth, short term real estate investments look like a no-brainer in hindsight but can often go overlooked, especially when you're busy growing your family. Even if it is a stretch, we knew we could be scrappy and overcome whatever adversity we encountered. We all possess that power deep inside ourselves. It is human nature to not want to lose that which we've gained. For that reason, you will always find a way, a way to cover that month's mortgage payment when finances are tight, or to replace the HVAC system unexpectedly. The thing that you can't make up for is time and we knew buying young would pay dividends later, both figuratively and literally.

With these thoughts seeded in our brains, we stayed curious and open-minded to opportunities that may come our way and just when we were on the cusp of our journey into parenthood and traditional suburban family life, we threw ourselves a curve ball. On a whim, we bought a small, but quaint cottage in Cape Cod as a vacation rental in our 3rd trimester. And that is when our detour into entrepreneurial life began and we didn't even know it.

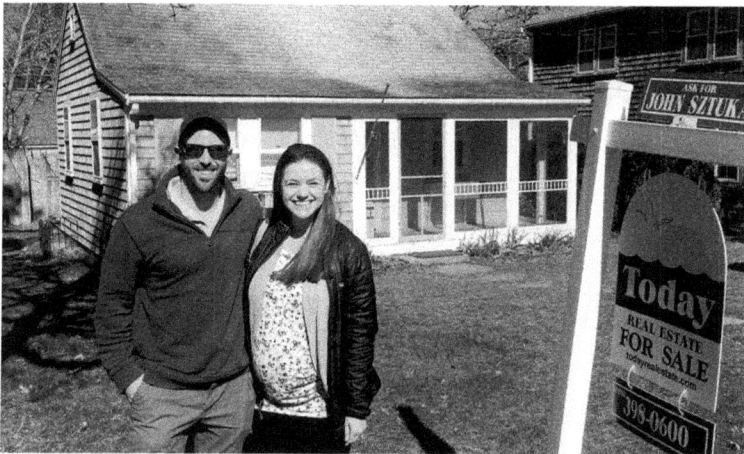

Dave and Kim, six months pregnant with their son Logan, closing on their first investment property in Dennis Port, Cape Cod in April 2019.

Cape Cod had been a vacation spot for us over the years and we had dreamed of buying a home there for ourselves. With our family growing, we had graduated from just crashing at friends' houses to actually renting a home ourselves starting that summer of 2019. We had set a goal of buying one by the time we were 35. We loved the idea of buying it when we were young, using it ourselves for a week or two per year and then renting it the rest of the season to cover the expenses and then having it paid off by retirement age. This just seemed like a smarter plan than paying someone else thousands of dollars for that one week vacation year after year. We'd rather that money in our pocket, actually having other people pay off our vacation home for us and ultimately having a tangible asset at the end of the day that we could leave to our kids.

Then one morning in February of 2019, Kim got to work early and decided to hop on Zillow for a couple minutes while enjoying her morning coffee. She had just finished her final grad school class at Bentley University the week before and was four months pregnant with our son, Logan. As with every venture, Kim wanted to start her research early and often so we could be well prepared by the time opportunity would strike for their Cape Cod vacation home rental. She did not expect to find a house under $300k, walking distance to the beach and boasting "strong rental history" in the first line of the listing that also had been sitting on the market for seven months. The less than five hundred square foot cottage built in 1930 was adorable and fun with bright pops of paint in every room and a cozy screened in front porch. She sent the listing to Dave and he said "let's go!" and we planned to attend the open house that weekend.

In typical New England fashion, there was seven inches of snow on the forecast for the Saturday morning of the open house. That didn't deter Dave at all and he insisted we still go. In hindsight, the conditions weren't that bad and we even got there early and did drive-bys of several other houses on the market. None of those had the same curb appeal or great location of this house, and they were all more expensive, further making the case that this was a great deal we had on our hands. We were the first ones at the open house, and actually the only ones to attend all day, we later found out. It was a comically brief tour since the house was so small, so we took it as an opportunity to ask the realtor a number of questions about himself, the rental history of the home and the sellers. When we hopped back into Dave's Jeep to head home, Dave turned to Kim and asked "What do you think?" and Kim said "I think we should go for it!".

Kim is typically not the spontaneous one of the two of us, so her being convinced that we had found "the home" for us sealed the deal. We started brainstorming names for the property and landed on Sunny Daze Cottage, after our first Great Dane Sunny, on that very drive home. We closed in April, and we had accomplished our goal five years earlier than our initial plan, a plan that we ourselves were cautiously optimistic would actually happen.

With our son due in three months and the peak summer season on the horizon, we quickly got to work to furnish, decorate, and stock the house with supplies and were live on Airbnb within a week. The cleaning company that had serviced the house the previous year said they could take on the house again, which was a huge relief as we were having trouble finding anyone who could do same day turnovers on Saturdays in the summer. We had friends and family book a stay the first few weekends and provide feedback on the house and things we had overlooked, and then we had our first real guests at the end of May. That stay went off without a hitch and bookings started rolling in for the rest of the summer now that we had a few positive reviews on our listing.

That first rental season has several learning curves for us to overcome with us getting familiar with the nuances of the

Airbnb platform, both of us messaging guests at the same time, and figuring out our systems with our cleaner for managing turnovers and supply ordering. We also were tested with our first natural disaster. A tornado had hit our house the week after our son was born. Tornadoes are rare for Cape Cod, so we were in disbelief when we first heard the news. Thankfully we had only minor damage, the house just lost power for a few hours and it only cost us a couple days of work cleaning up branches and debris. Aside from the tornado, there were minor speed bumps through it all, but that summer was largely a success as we met our revenue goals and made enough to cover all expenses until the next rental season. We were proud of ourselves as we kicked up our heels at the end of the season and prepared to address some deferred maintenance and improvements to the home, while also relishing in the fact we didn't have to worry about much guest communication for the next several months.

ONE AND DONE - NOT SO FAST

Going into purchasing Sunny Daze Cottage, we really believed this was a *one and done* deal. We had bought smart, forecasted our income and expenses appropriately, and proved we were capable of self-managing the property. We were giving ourselves a pat on the back for taking a risk of acquiring a second home, a second mortgage, and all that comes along with it because of the upside of free vacations for ourselves for the coming years, the tax benefits, and the equity growth. We knew that our next several years would be tied up with a heavy focus on our growing family and that it gets a lot harder to carve out time and money for learning, exploring, and pulling the trigger on these kinds of ventures. It wasn't until we took a trip down to the cottage during that off season and listened to the audio-book of *Rich Dad, Poor Dad* by Robert Kiyosaki during the car ride that we contemplated doing more of this thing called real estate investing. That book really opened our eyes to the fact that we were trading time for money and would be a slave to that reality for the next several decades unless we made a drastic change and started acquiring more income producing assets. Kiyosaki promotes real estate as a great asset class to invest in and that there are a variety of ways to do so. This contrarian thinking to how we were taught to measure achievement through academic success and W2 jobs, chasing titles, salaries and benefits packages, helped push our thinking into what more we could do in this space.

Figuring out our next move took time and the COVID-19 pandemic added an unforeseen stall to everything. That winter of 2019 to 2020 We were considering getting a mountain house in Maine as we had been vacationing there for a number of years as well and learned that we could do a ten percent down loan on second homes, a fact we'd wished we'd known when we bought Sunny Daze Cottage. We couldn't use that type of loan to buy another Cape house because that would automatically be assumed to be an investment home, require at least twenty percent down and be subject to higher interest rates. We could, however, leverage it for a completely different market that underwriters would find reasonable, like wanting a beach house for the summer and ski house for winter.

We'd planned to repeat the formula we'd used with Sunny Daze, get some personal use out of the home and rent it the rest of the time as an investment. There were some gorgeous homes on the market at reasonable prices, but we lacked funding at the time to source a down payment, furnishings and reserves to get started so we put that idea on the back burner for a while.

Shortly after hitting the pause button on our mountain home search, the COVID-19 pandemic was upon us and we found ourselves working overtime at our jobs in our 1500 square foot home with an eight month old baby that had just learned to crawl. Daycare closed down for sixteen straight weeks, so we were left to figure out how to balance work, childcare, and the upcoming rental season for Sunny Daze. We had family members willing to help with our son, but it was tricky to navigate given the guidelines to social distance from others before vaccines were developed. On top of that, we had a fully booked calendar for the summer and were unsure of the fate of the upcoming rental season. Would governments allow travel? Even if they do, will guests want to cancel? We began to pad our reserve fund for Sunny Daze just in case. We were also optimistically excited about spending the whole summer at the beach ourselves if our rental season was a complete dud.

Dave and Kim enjoying a day trip to Truro Vineyards for wine tasting during with 2020 Cape Cod vacation.

Much to our surprise, the rental season exploded with demand. Governments did impose some rules on travel and quarantines so we had some out of state guests cancel, but those open dates booked up insanely fast. One night, we had a guest cancel their one week stay in July at 11 pm and we woke up the next morning to six booking requests and countless messages from prospective guests impatiently awaiting our reply. Since people were working from home, more shoulder season stays and weekdays bookings came in. Restaurants wisely responded to the health guidelines by adding more outdoor seating, switching to virtual menus accessed by QR codes and amping up their online ordering and takeout options. We decided to up our vacation time down there from one week to two weeks given the burnout we were feeling, and we arrived in mid-June ecstatic for our vacation. It turned out to be our best one yet.

That trip consisted of our first use of our off-roading beach pass to Crowes Pasture, arguably one of the best beaches you'll find in New England. Foodies at heart, we dined out at restaurants for the first in months. Our son, weeks away from his first birthday, got to enjoy playing in the sand at Sea Street Beach and rides in his bike stroller cruising around the neighborhood. We had perfect weather the entire time and got to see friends and family throughout the two weeks. Disappointed to leave, we vowed that one day in a few short years we'd make it so we could spend the entire summer here like many of our neighbors do.

LONG DISTANCE INVESTING ADVENTURES

In early 2021, Dave had started studying for his real estate license and looking into real estate investing out of state. By the summer, he had secured his first "BRRRR" (Buy Rehab Rent Refinance Repeat) investment in Chattanooga, TN and partnered with another investor to ultimately form another LLC and BRRRR several more deals. This venture into long-term rentals was the first time where we were not both in the driver's seat of the journey. At this time, we were going through In Vitro Fertilization treatments to have a second child and Kim was fully supportive of Dave pursuing this avenue of real estate investing, but she wanted to be minimally involved so she could focus on their toddler, fertility treatments and eventually a successful pregnancy.

Chattanooga was an adventure and an opportunity to learn, and though the investment strategy differed from what we had been accustomed to with short-term rentals in Cape Cod, it provided a relatively safe opportunity to exercise new real estate investing muscles. At the heart of it, investing 1000 miles away, while conducting renovations, managing budgets, and partnering with property managers offered opportunities to develop new skills, which little did we know, would serve critical in building future businesses of ours. Let's dig into that for a moment.

When embarking on the Chattanooga journey, the first skill that we needed to develop was our networking skillset. This was a critical piece of our success. Networking was the tool that we leveraged to learn about the local market and understand who the big players were for realtors, contractors, lenders, property managers, and other investors - all of whom we hoped to bring value to. Establishing a consistent networking strategy in this market was fundamental to our success. Again, a skillset that has led to more success which you'll learn later in this chapter.

Through this experience, we learned of new financing strategies from other investors and we learned how the world of hard money and construction loans work. One thing I'd like to point out is that the investors and operators who rise to the top understand that anything is possible in this industry if you are creative enough. We've had deals fall apart 5 days before closing due to challenges with a lender, but, because of our network, we were introduced to new lenders who were able to get the deal closed in less than 72 hours, saving us thousands of dollars. The lesson here was to be prepared for anything and never stop growing your network.

Beyond financing, we learned how to build and manage a team, with a careful system of checks and balances. This sounds far easier than it actually is. To be successful, you have to understand the motivation of all of your team members. You need to understand and be keenly aware of what "winning" looks like to them and make sure that all members of the team are motivated and engaged. We learned how to create a positive, supportive, and trusting environment for all team members so together, we could all accomplish the goal of closing a deal, getting a home renovated, and finding a great tenant. This takes practice, boy it takes practice and once you get good at it, your opportunities and value in this industry skyrocket.

Networking, financing strategies and managing a team were the biggest skills learned through investing in long-term rentals in Chattanooga, TN and were assets to leverage in the next steps of our short-term rental journey.

FALLING INTO A FAMILY OF 4

In the Fall of 2021, Dave completed his real estate courses and passed the real estate license test in Massachusetts just before we welcomed our beautiful and healthy baby girl, Brooke. Our lives were chaotic to say the least as we learned to juggle a newborn and a toddler. We also had to adjust our roles in how we managed Sunny Daze Cottage and find pockets of time for Dave to work on lead generation for his real estate sales business now that he was an agent while also working full time as a director at a healthcare consulting firm. When we first launched Sunny Daze Cottage, we were both messaging guests, sometimes at the same time confusing the guest which we now laugh about. We eventually fell into a groove with just Kim messaging guests for a couple years. By the time Brooke arrived and with Dave being gone for large blocks of time on weekends working at his brokerage's office, we decided to shift to having Dave lead on all guest communication and cleaner coordination. Dave will even admit that those tasks weren't his strong suit, but he would try his best and Kim had to learn to not let perfection be the enemy of good.

It became important to re-evaluate and adjust our roles and duties along the way. We each learned to delegate to the other and let go of how we would do something differently. If the outcome was good enough to propel us forward, then let it go. If you couldn't relinquish that control, then you should be the primary owner. We also try to create opportunities for each of us to cater to our strengths and do what we enjoy most. There are still plenty of things that just have to get done that neither of us enjoy, so our strategy for those was to eventually outsource those.

What Dave truly enjoys in this business is sales. Sales is a passion of Dave's through and through, but it's not "the chase" for Dave. It's the ability to help others achieve their goals that Dave truly enjoys. When it comes to sales, Dave has always thrived in helping his clients achieve their goals in selling or buying. On the buying front, he often serves as a consultant, particularly for short-term rental investor clients. He's their fiduciary to ensure they are making the right purchase and that the home will be in alignment with their financial goals. This act of service has become an all in passion of Dave's. It is not always easy though. This line of business is terribly inconsistent and it will one hundred percent eat into your personal and family time due to the nature of the work, all big learning curves for Dave and Kim.

There were several activities that Dave was able to conduct to help him build his sales business and brand - all of which was through marketing. Marketing in itself is its own skillset. But what do you market? Well, Dave decided to share all that he had learned from his Chattanooga investments. There was a world of knowledge to tap into here. From analyzing deals, learning different ways to finance them, traps to avoid, negotiating deals, all of these were valuable skills learned in Chattanooga that Dave was able to leverage to build his client base. Clients wanted to tap into that knowledge and it blossomed into a business that helped clients achieve their goal of buying a home!

The first time the whole family came up to Logan's Lodge
for a vacation in October 2022.

Around this time, our idea of buying a mountain house had boomeranged back on to our radar and this time we were equipped with more knowledge and buying power to pull the trigger on the right home. Both our primary home and Sunny Daze Cottage had handsomely appreciated during the COVID housing boom so we were able to take out lines of credit against our homes to use for investing. We also discovered tools like AirDNA which can show you how well certain Airbnbs are performing in an area. We had checked the tool against Sunny Daze Cottage to see how accurate it was and it was spot on which gave us confidence in the tool and we used it to explore markets in Maine and New Hampshire. Dave had also learned some lead generation strategies from his courses and peers to drum up off-market deals which he could use both for clients and our mountain house hunt. Finding off-market deals means engaging in various forms of outreach to owners of homes that match your buyer's criteria for houses not currently for sale. If you hit the right prospective seller at the right time, that's where the magic can happen. All of these ingredients blended into the perfect, ripe opportunity for us when owners of a home in Bethel, ME actually responded to a letter Dave wrote them. The home was on the market a couple years earlier and the owners had found the home too difficult to manage in their older age and they had not used the home as much as they had expected to.

Our mountain home, which we named Logan's Lodge, allowed us to apply three strong years of STR operator experience in Cape Cod, to a new home in a new market. Of course, there were new learning curves, such as a new guest demographic, more amenities to maintain (a hot tub and generator), a deeper level of design, more service people to manage, and new seasons to manage through. What helped tremendously was the skills acquired in Chattanooga for building and managing a team. With Logan's Lodge being a three and a half hour drive away, we couldn't go there on a whim if there were issues. Trips to that market had to be well thought out and calculated.

By taking three years of experience in the industry and putting all into this home, very quickly Dave and Kim were seeing a high volume of bookings come in. It was exciting and nerve racking at the same time. With many more systems and processes required for Logan's Lodge, it was exciting seeing everything come together allowing Dave and Kim to provide an amazing vacation experience for the guests. We'll admit, there had been several instances where we had considered outsourcing the property management of their short-term rentals. It can be a daunting task and often times guests reach out about the simplest things but at the worst times (bath time for kids, client calls, etc.). The challenge though was every time we spoke with a property manager, we felt as though they could never hit our same revenue numbers and they wanted to take an extraordinary commission, so we began reading books such as *Short Term Rental, Long Term Wealth* by Avery Carl, listening to Podcasts, and learning how we could systematize our business to be more profitable, yet take less time to manage. All of these learnings we put into practice with our existing properties.

Things started to dovetail between Dave's real estate agent sales and our short-term rental management experience when Dave started getting clients interested in buying and having us rent their home for them. People were seeing his content on social media about our Airbnbs, properties he had gotten under contract for clients and sharing his knowledge and addressing frequently asked questions through a new podcast he had launched, Hassle Free RE.

This spurred interest ranging from friends Dave hadn't talked to in twenty years simply asking for advice to serious buyer clients wanting Dave to represent them. Dave could service the sales needs as an agent in the state of Massachusetts or analyst running numbers for deals in states he wasn't licensed for, but managing others rental homes was a net new skillset that ultimately led to the forming of The 5 Star Co-Host business. In the beginning Kim wasn't much involved in the business or even the podcast, but his solo venture pretty quickly morphed into a partnership with Kim being involved in both and us taking on the ventures ahead as a team. Next, we'll share more details about how our partnership in life became a partnership in business.

*Dave and Kim recording a podcast before heading to dinner
for their five year wedding anniversary.*

THE BUSINESS

As we reflected on our journey going into business together, we realized that our story follows a common model you typically learn about in business classes in college, Tuckman's stages of group formation. Tuckman proposed that groups go through the phases of forming, storming, norming and performing as they mature, strengthen relationships and learn to collaborate better. We have gone through all of these phases and even revert back to some as we encounter new challenges and enter new levels of growth and success. We now want to share some stories that demonstrate each of these phases and how we overcame them.

FORMING OUR BUSINESS

Forming the 5 Star Co-Host was a gradual process over several months before we were both fully onboard with growing it to a substantial level. In late 2022, Dave had taken on management of a couple Airbnb properties for friends and clients he had sold vacation homes to. He had established the LLC as a sole

141

proprietorship and was running this business as a side hustle to his work as an agent with little involvement by Kim at the time. Management of Airbnbs for other owners is known as "co-hosting" in the business and Dave hadn't ever considered doing co-hosting until he had gone to the STR Wealth Conference in June 2022. At the end of that conference, the sponsors had announced a smaller, more intimate retreat in Miami in September of that year. Dave proposed the idea to Kim and we jumped at the opportunity to have a mini-vacation, keep the post-conference high going and learn even more from others in the industry. Kim had a bit of FOMO not being at the conference, and in fact had spent the few days Dave was gone running around to our two personal properties, which are five hours apart, to clean and prep for guests as a cleaner had ghosted us.

That STR Wealth Retreat in September proved to be worth its weight in gold as it opened Kim's eyes to co-hosting and we got to see some incredible case studies of the life changing effects a co-hosting business can have from some of the speakers at the conference. Most of all, we were able to be in the same room and in parallel, work on our mind set and goal setting together. Dave had returned from the June conference with big ideas and thought-provoking questions on growing income, acquiring weather, and how we wanted to live our lives. Kim quite literally rolled her eyes at the ideas and questions as there was admittedly a gap in where her head was at in comparison to Dave's. The retreat helped close that gap and Dave continued to get traction with more co-hosting leads coming in as we entered 2023.

The organizers of the September retreat each had a mastermind of which we got to meet many members of at the retreat, and in January 2023 we joined the STR Secrets Mastermind led by Mike Sjogren. Since we had gotten a crash course of material from the masterminds in the content of the presentations in Miami and we had created a plethora of networking connections, we didn't see the need to join the mastermind just yet. Cost was also a big consideration. We knew how much other members had paid to join and were unclear if the cost for a couple to join was in fact double that. We also told ourselves that once we reach a certain level of success on our own, then we can afford to join. We absolutely recognize that thinking was backwards. Stretching to make the investment could help us reach our goal faster. Our reservations were rooted in fear and a scarcity mindset was plaguing us at that time.

The remedy to a scarcity mindset is re-framing your thoughts, and we find that connection and taking action helps us do just that. It couldn't hurt to ask what the cost really is for a couple to join the mastermind. And if it was truly double the cost, then why not invest in just one of us joining for now and sharing all the resources and tools together. Kim reached out to set up a call with the Mastermind team on New Years Day and we joined a week later. We felt ecstatic and proud for taking a vote of confidence in ourselves to invest like this in a mastermind. It also truly felt like a homecoming as we knew quite a few people in the group already. The moment we joined the mastermind together solidified our forming our business as a team and that we were truly committed to making our co-hosting business a raving success.

STORMS AHEAD

Our business and partnership quickly hit some intense turbulence and caused us to pause and seriously reconsider the feasibility of us chartering this business together. The thing about hospitality businesses and dealing with short-term rentals is that this business can bring out the best in people, but it can also bring out the worst in people, of guests and owners alike. We also learned that we have opposing styles of how we react to conflict in our business which can serve us well in some situations and can be our Achilles' heel in others.

What got us through some tough situations at that time was staying rooted in our values, learning about our individual styles of dealing with conflict, and setting boundaries. We strive to stay reasonable, classy and professional in the face of adversity. We feel that if we always strive to embody those characteristics, we can endure any challenge and sleep at night knowing that we handled the situation as best we could given the circumstances. We can't control how others behave. All we can do is control how we react to it. The words of Michelle Obama, "when they go low, we go high" really became a motto of ours during that period and continues to be a guiding force in how we do business.

Next, we set and actually enforced boundaries, with ourselves and our customers. We'd encourage everyone at the onset of a business venture, if you only do one thing, then please do this because it will save you a world of headache. Since Dave was running the day-to-day operations and Kim was unavailable while at her full-time job, we agreed on criteria and at what threshold things should be escalated to being a joint decision on how to handle something. Dave is quick to react and take action, whereas Kim is pensive and reflective. Swift reaction is great for situations like when we have a displaced guest and need new accommodations for them, and Dave resolves that on the fly. Careful calculation of how to handle a volatile guest or an owner transitioning on or off of working with us is where Kim provides thoughtful guidance to try to assuage tempers and deliver reasonable outcomes for all parties.

There were times where these two opposing styles clashed and that was some real storming we had to work through to get back on a unified front. This is where boundaries came in. Boundaries are setting limits and communicating consequences for pushing that limit. If that limit gets crossed, then you follow through with the aforementioned consequence. It is binary. What is also helpful is a warning light, that the boundary hasn't been hit yet but you're uncomfortable with where things are headed. So, we also started to communicate when the warning light was going up, and these tools of communication have greatly helped us create a more docile environment for our business.

SMOOTH SAILING

The next stage of group development is norming, reaching a stage of productivity as everyone understands and performs their roles and responsibilities well. This is the stage that felt like a breath of fresh air after a rocky couple months of learning, storming and growing. Our biggest propellers to get us into this stage were hiring help, adding structure and continuing to learn.

Pretty quickly after joining the STR Secrets Mastermind, we hired a virtual assistant and then a second a couple months later. We always planned to hire a team of assistants to handle guest communication with plans to even support 24/7 coverage eventually so that responsibility wasn't purely on our shoulders. We covered that cost out of our own pocket initially because we saw it as an investment in the future of the business and wanted to onboard them before both our client base grew significantly and before the busy summer season was upon us. We also wanted to ensure that we protected time with our kids as much as we could.

Having a one year old and three year old greatly affects how we make each and every decision in the business. If we were young and scrappy in our 20s, we'd probably have held off on hiring assistants for a while longer to keep that money in our pocket, but we're at a stage in our lives where we continue to make investments to trade money for time back so we can cherish this time with our family. It is a balancing act, saving and spending, using our time vs. others times to accomplish tasks in our business, but overall we are looking to off load more and more so we can work on our business instead of in it and so we can maximize quality time with our family, because in the end that is who we're doing all of this for.

With growing our team, we added structure with heavy documentation, standing meetings, and key performance indicator (KPI) reviews. Documentation was paramount to get our knowledge out of our heads and into referenceable guidance for our growing team. We created baseline documentation of things like standard operating procedures (SOPs) which are essentially how-to guides for all the basic tasks in our business. Now our team references and updates those existing SOPs as processes evolve and they create new ones.

We all join a weekly team meeting on Mondays and a monthly strategy meeting on Fridays. In those meetings we have a series of metrics we review related to our pipeline, current client base and the performance of our current properties. These check-ins are equally productive and invigorating. The consistency and predictability of these facets of the business helped us reach a good place of calmness and sustainability faster than we had expected.

PEAK PERFORMANCE

Dave, Kim and Jodie Stirling at the March 2023 book launch party in Nashville TN for the Hospitable Host 2 book in which Dave & Kim were featured as one of the 40 stories of Airbnb hosts from around the world.

The last stage of team formation is performing, and it is far too soon to declare ourselves as victorious at this stage but we are proud of the significant progress we are making towards our goals. Our boutique co-hosting operation is steadily growing. At the time of print, we have eighteen properties expected to gross over $1.4mm in annual revenue after less than six months in our mastermind. We are constantly revisiting our processes to balance quality and scalability and weed out any inefficiencies. We are frequently soliciting feedback from our team on areas of improvement or opportunity. We are insatiably consuming all of the continuing education we can get our hands on whether it's re-watching training from our mastermind, reading books like Mike Michalowicz's *Clockwork*, listening to podcasts or connecting with our peers and coach. We then try to apply those learnings, master them, then repeat the cycle of learn-apply-master. We carve out time for reflection and conversations around growth, vision and strategy with just the two of us as captains of this ship.

Through our reflection efforts, combined twenty plus years of professional experience, and voracious appetite for knowledge we try to identify things we need to be doing to be among the greatest and most successful companies. For example, we have established a mission statement and a set of core values, cornerstones of the best companies in the world. Our mission statement for The 5 Star Co-Host is:

Enjoyable vacations for everyone.

This mission resonated with us because it applies to every relationship our business touches. Guests want to have an enjoyable stay in a home that feels like their own that makes them want to come back year after year. Owners want to be stress-free and achieve their personal and financial goals with their home. Vendors want to enjoy working with a business partner that is organized, kind, professional and that pays on time. And we want our team to enjoy working at The 5 Star Co-Host. When you enjoy where you work and who you work with, the whole team performs at a higher level and that enjoyment carries through in your interactions with guests, owners and vendors alike.

Folding into our mission statement are our core values. We have built these slowly over time and continue to evolve them as we encounter obstacles in our business and determine how we want to carry ourselves as we face those challenges. As of today, our core values are:

- "Our goal is to get better, not bigger. If we get better, [bigger will come]."
- We pay people on time.
- Always assume good intent.

The first core value: getting better, not bigger came from a podcast with Stephen Kircher, CEO and President of Boyne Resorts that owns several major US ski resorts including Sunday River, the ski mountain nearest to Logan's Lodge. Boyne Resorts is making hefty investments into their ski resorts such as cutting-edge technologies for snow making, top of the line chair lifts with heated seats, major trail expansion, and expansion of parking lots and shuttle services, just to name a few. He is at the helm of a family business of over seventy years and you can tell he truly enjoys and cares about the experience his customers have at his ski resorts when you hear him in interviews. He is a skier himself and frequents his own ski resorts, but also ventures out to resorts across Europe to help get inspiration for his business.

The reason we wanted to share all of this is because it exemplifies a business owner that truly cares about the customer experience and is not afraid of enormous investments in his business to further augment the customer experience. That's exactly how we want to be. That focus on the right things, quality, doing right by guests and continuous improvement, comes back around to benefit you and your business in the long run and the cycle repeats.

Our second core value: of paying people on time sounds simple and obvious, but we have seen instances of these being completely disregarded and for that reason we wanted to bring it in as a core value. There are a lot of monetary transactions in a short-term rental business. As a simple example, a guest pays Airbnb, who then pays you as the co-host, then you pay the cleaner, then you pay the owner at the end of every month and you keep your management fee. Anything we have control over, we pay promptly. Because paying promptly builds trust. Trust is built off of countless small actions aggregated over time.

We feel it is incredibly important to build up this good

will early. This trust reservoir then helps you if you get behind because you and your whole family were sick that week. Or you got behind while you were traveling to assist with new house launches. Trust affords you grace in these scenarios, and we extend that same grace to others in these reciprocal relationships we have built.

Our third core value: of assuming good intent could be said another way; there are two sides to every story. We try to see the good in everyone and assume that any action someone has taken was not executed on with any ill will. There are a lot of players and a lot of moving parts in a short-term rental business, so it can be easy to jump to conclusions.

We try to pause, take a breath, assume the other party had good intent and a valid reason for doing what they did, and then diplomatically get their side of the story. This applies to everyone we interact with: individuals on our team, vendors, guests and owners. This is also an incredibly helpful approach to have in our personal lives as a couple and as parents.

Our mission statement is designed to be a steady north star for us as our co-hosting business continues to evolve, and we expect our core values to evolve with it. An important part of the performing stage is continuous learning and we consider ourselves lifelong learners that are never done, never reaching a plateau, never kicking back and getting comfortable. These guiding principles of our business not only anchor the team, but anchor us as a couple and as co-founders of The 5 Star Co-Host. Having artifacts like this that live outside of ourselves and our brains has allowed us to better articulate why we are in business and how we do business.

WHAT'S NEXT

One might argue that the last stage of Tuckman's stages of group formation is adjourning, the dissolving of the group either because the goal has been completed or the group is no longer chasing that goal. An example of adjourning is when your group for your class project has submitted their final assignment and the semester is over. In business, adjourning can take many forms. It can mean going out of business. It can mean selling the business. It can mean merging businesses. It can mean getting acquired by a larger business. We do know people like Julie George, author of *Million Dollar Host*, who have exited their co-hosting business by selling it and are incredibly happy with that decision and what they're doing now.

We have discussed our long-term goals for ourselves and The 5 Star Co-Host, but have absolutely no plans of exiting so this phase is dormant for us for now. Do we see ourselves co-hosting into our 80s and leaving the business to our kids? Absolutely not, we say with a chuckle.

We have some *BIG* aspirations for our business and personal investments that others would say are near impossible, but we know better. Having a big vision and taking massive action is what's going to get us there. And we aren't waiting to start giving back. From the very first dollar we've earned with the co-hosting business, we've started donating ten percent of our income to charity.

An abundance mindset and practicing gratitude are things we are honestly working on each and every day ourselves. An abundance mindset is not natural to most and just like a muscle, it will atrophy if you don't exercise it.

As we shared earlier, "Our goal is to get better, not bigger. If we get better, [bigger will come]" and our KPIs are indicating we are getting both bigger and better, and we plan to ride that wave. We do plan to continue to level up ourselves so we spend

151

less and less time IN the business and have more recreational time with each other and maximize time with our kids over the next one and half decades before they leave home.

We'll know when the time is right for us to firm up a succession plan, but for now we'll continue to focus and mastermind around how we can be better and let a succession plan reveal itself over time in our reflection and masterminding conversations. For this reason, the performance stage is our finish line and the sky is the limit on how far we can take our co-hosting business and help more and more owners maximize their investments and guests enjoy an incredible and memorable vacation.

Sunny Daze was absolutely all and more of what we expected!! Sparkling clean, and all the comforts of home! Exceptional amenities included and tastefully decorated. Grounds were very relaxing and enjoyable. Outside shower was awesome!! Location was quiet and peaceful, and close to many restaurants and shops. Would definitely recommend Sunny Daze to folks visiting the Cape!

—Guest of Sunny Daze Cottage, June 2023

DAVE AND KIM'S QUICK TIPS

As we go on year five of our real estate investment journey, we'd like to share a few tips and tricks we've learned along the way.

Action: Do one activity towards achieving your goal every day. These can be small, like taking five minutes to read an article online, listening to a twenty minute podcast, or attending a whole day conference. Action creates momentum. Action leads to outcomes. Action can also help you get lucky when preparation meets opportunity. On that February day that Kim was browsing Zillow, she was taking action. She knew that browsing over months or years would make her good at knowing when a killer deal came on the market. Touring houses would further assist in determining a good deal. It also would make the dream more real. You'll find many of the most successful people in the world attest to outstanding results being achieved through visualization exercises.

Deploying all of your sensory memory towards a goal, an outcome can greatly help you acquire it. If you really want a sports car, test drive one, ride in a friend's sports car, closing your eyes and mentally bringing yourself back there.

- What did it smell like?
- What color was the interior?
- How did the clutch feel in your hand?

Triggering all your senses to make it feel real all help drive your subconscious to work with you in achieving it. We think this is incredibly important with vacation homes. Getting out and touring open houses. Renting one similar to what you want, or even one that's a stretch for you. Take action in a variety of ways towards your goal.

Explore: There are a variety of financing options out there for funding an investment and a plethora of investment options. If you're truly serious about getting started or continuing in real estate investing in general, or a specific facet of it, start talking to lenders, listen to podcasts by experienced investors and take a serious look at what assets you have at your disposal to throw at this venture.

- Do you get an annual bonus you can save?
- Do you have home equity you can tap into?
- A car you don't use or need that you can sell?

After we purchased our small cottage on Cape Cod, we thought we were tapped out for a good ten years because we'd have to penny pinch to save up for another down payment of twenty percent while paying a small fortune for daycare. We didn't know about mortgage lenders offering ten percent down for second homes. We didn't know much about home equity lines of credit (HELOCs) except that most people took them out to get an addition on their primary home. Do your homework and don't be afraid to be vulnerable. There is no dumb question.

Practice Patience: Success takes time and you'll rack up a lot of mistakes along the way. If you take those mistakes and learn from them, you'll improve quicker rather than going slow, methodical and trying to be perfect so you can avoid any pain. You'll also encounter new mistakes that further accelerate your progress. We find that if we are running into the same problem repeatedly, then we're doing something wrong and not learning from it. The quicker we learn from it, address it systemically and move on, the faster we climb. Mistakes are inevitable and a part of learning. We have given ourselves grace and allowed ourselves to be vulnerable about our mistakes. It can also be easy to compare to others further in their journey. Books like

Dan Sullivan's *The Gap and The Gain* have helped us reframe our thinking around that and measure our success from where WE were six months ago, a year ago, five years ago.

Learn Together: We take the same rigor to learning about relationships, communication and parenting as we do to learning about business and real estate. When one of us finds a great resource on a particular topic we share it with the other. That shared learning helps us ensure our knowledge gap never gets too wide. It helps spur great intellectual discussion and thoughtful reflection. And just like we find with business materials, we find we have to revisit those same great resources over and over again to sharpen those skills or take in more from that material with each review. This has helped us continue to learn more about ourselves and each other even ten years into our relationship.

Good Intent: Just as always assuming good intent is one of our business core values, it is one we adopt with our relationship as a couple. We try to approach conflict with curiosity, a yearning to understand the other person's side. Giving enough time and space to hear each person's thoughts and sentiments without interruption is still not something we're perfect at, but we find conversations go much better when we do approach them this way. It is easy to not bring our best foot forward when we're tired, stressed, overwhelmed and putting our needs last ahead of our kids.

Grace, empathy and listening to understand are our antidote to conflict and frustration.

Functionality: Our number one tip for STRs is to not overlook functionality. It can be easy to get caught up with the fun of planning accent walls and purchasing throw pillows, or arranging for big ticket amenities like a hot tub, but we find that people often overlook the basics like having enough trash barrels for twelve guests staying a full week. Or thinking about where a guest will want to plug in their phone to charge overnight while they sleep. We encourage owners to really pay attention to these details when guests stay at their house, or for co-hosts, to at a minimum role play what a typical day will look like for a guest so you can iron out all of those usability kinks.

- When you wake up and go to make coffee, can you find the coffee filters? The mugs?
- Do you provide cream and sugar packets or do you instruct guests to bring those?

Trialing your vacation home for usability is important before you have even your first guest, and then to revisit every few months to create and maintain an enjoyable vacation for guests.

How Can We Help You

First and foremost, we want to help people acquire their first STR vacation home to own. Many people say they want a vacation home, dream of owning one, but never get around to pulling the trigger on it. We want to help those people actually take the leap. We provide resources on our podcast, Hassle Free RE, to help first time home buyers of STRs.

If there is a topic you don't see covered but would like to see, then please message us on our social media and we'll look to add it to the line up!

Secondly, we can manage your vacation home with a level of care and attention that is unmatched by the big, national property managers in your area. The 5 Star Co-Host is a boutique, luxury vacation home management company. We are your marketing partner, your pricing strategists, your consultants. We are making daily optimizations for our rental properties. We are deploying all of the latest technologies and strategies to get eyeballs on your home and ultimately people in the door at a competitive price for your market. We care for your homes like they are our own. Our list of current areas we are serving can be found on our website, WWW.5STRCOHOST.COM.

SPONTANEOUS FUN

As overachievers each in our own right with triple duty jobs to do between our management company, Kim's full-time job and parents to two toddlers, we are finding we need to force ourselves to take our foot off the gas pedal, relax and be present way more often. Our favorite moments lately have been last minute plans to enjoy a margarita and a meal out with our kids on a Friday night, having a throwback movie night of Wedding Crashers after the kids go to bed even though we've both been up since 4 AM, or enjoying some wine and a prolonged game of Scrabble as we both, competitive by nature, scour our Scrabble dictionaries to find THE best word for our turn. We can be extremely disciplined and calculated with our schedules and routines. We are people who are early to bed, early to rise. We take a couple hours to work or work out before the kids get up to squeeze every last ounce of productivity out of the day.

Every once in a while, we need to shake things up with something spontaneous and a bit counterproductive to our goals just because it puts a smile on our face and fosters connection. Our schedules and routines often get thrown off kilter with something related to the kids, like a late bedtime, a nap time cut short or a kid being home sick from school, so we've had to learn to be adaptable and adjust our productivity expectations. Something feels nice about having this curveball be one we gave ourselves and for a fun reason, enjoying good food, drinks and laughs just because life is short and tomorrow is never guaranteed.

Brooke, Kim, Logan and Dave at Sunny Daze Cottage for their annual family vacation in July 2023.

Scan the QR code below to watch
our interview on Youtube!

ACKNOWLEDGMENTS

From Dave & Kim Menapace

Dave and Kim would like to thank their friends and families for supporting them throughout their entrepreneur and real estate journey. Support takes many forms, from thoughtful concern and questions coming from a place of love to full blown cheerleading, screaming from the stands. This road comes with its own speed bumps and curve balls, and we appreciate all of the love, support and time people have put into us and to helping with childcare so that we can learn to overcome those challenges to propel our dreams forward. We've had our highs and certainly had our lows throughout this journey, and the truest and most genuine relationships have revealed themselves through it all. In this space, we've also gotten to form new friendships with people that now feel like family and for that we are truly grateful.

Lastly, we want to acknowledge our amazing children, Logan and Brooke. You each have a unique and beautiful spirit. We appreciate your patience as we learn and grow as parents and as ambitious entrepreneurs. You ground us and remind us why we're doing all of this in the first place. You challenge us to be present, even when it's tough and we work in a business that doesn't sleep, and your smiles light up our world. Thank you and we love you so much.

ABOUT THE AUTHORS:
Dave & Kim Menapace

Dave and Kim are real estate investors, best-selling authors of The Hospitable Host Volume 2, co-founders of The 5 Star Co-Host vacation rental management company, and hosts of the Hassle Free RE podcast. Dave and Kim have been guest speakers on notable podcasts in the real estate space, including STR Secrets and The Boostly Podcast. Dave has been a guest speaker at various events and panels, including the 2023 STR Wealth Conference in Nashville.

Dave and Kim have a combined 25 years of business experience, Dave in healthcare, data analytics and consulting and Kim in strategy, software development, and marketing. In 2019, they purchased their first short-term rental, a tiny beach cottage in Cape Cod. That purchase led to the purchase of a second vacation home, several long-term rental investment properties, a career change for Dave, and the start of a successful Airbnb management company in 2022.

Dave is now a real estate investor, agent, and consultant and helps others analyze, purchase, and maximize revenue on their vacation homes. He's been able to apply his knowledge from his data analytics background to his deal analysis and Airbnb listing optimization. Kim works full time at a tech company in Boston and applies her strategy, project management and operations experience from the corporate world to their co-hosting business.

The 5 Star Co-Host is a boutique vacation home rental

company managing primarily high-end luxury homes in the New England and Chattanooga, TN areas. With 18 properties at the time of print, Dave and Kim purposely keep their portfolio small and intimate so they can deliver top notch customer service to both guests and owners alike.

Dave and Kim use their Hassle Free RE podcast and YouTube channel to share content and resources to help others recognize their dream of owning a short-term rental.

You can reach Dave and Kim and access their content through their linktree site!

HTTPS://LINKTR.EE/MENAPACE_REALESTATE

YOUR NETWORK IS YOUR NET WORTH

Andrew, Ryan and Dave at the 2023 Hospitable Hosts
Vol 2 Book Launch in Nashville TN

2023 Summer Couples Wealth & Health Retreat in New Hampshire (from left to right): Ryan, Shae, Dave, Kim, Meghan, Andrew, Steve, Christine, Eric Sicsko and Bridget Sicsko

Dave, Kim, Meghan and Andrew along with Hospitable Hosts Vol 1 & 2 Authors at the 2023 STR Wealth Conference in Nashville TN

Cash Street Advisors Press is committed to empowering authors like you to embark on an extraordinary publishing journey through sharing stories of financial and time freedom. Our mission is to bring these stories to life and provide them with the platform they deserve.

What sets us apart is our commitment to being more than just a publishing house. We're your partners, your cheerleaders, and your guides as you navigate the path to becoming a published author. Our team is dedicated to nurturing your literary ambitions and helping you shape a brighter future through your words.

Don't wait for the right moment—create it. Your story deserves to be told, and we're here to help you tell it in the most impactful way possible. Ready to get started?

Visit **WWW.CASHSTREETTECH.COM/CASHSTREETPRESS**
and begin your authorial adventure today!

www.ingramcontent.com/pod-product-compliance
Lightning Source LLC
Chambersburg PA
CBHW071418210326
41597CB00020B/3553